The Wales TUC, 1

The Wales TUC, 1974–2004

DEVOLUTION AND INDUSTRIAL POLITICS

By

JOE ENGLAND

UNIVERSITY OF WALES PRESS
CARDIFF
2004

British Library Cataloguing-in-Publication Data.
A catalogue record for this book is available from the British Library.

ISBN 0–7083–1919–X

Printed by Cromwell Press Ltd, Trowbridge, Wiltshire.

Contents

List of Illustrations   vii

Preface   ix

Acknowledgements   xiii

List of Abbreviations   xv

1   All Change   1

2   The Confrontation   17

3   A Campaigning Organization   37

4   The Enemy Within?   58

5   New Directions   80

6   Devolution and After   102

Notes   121

Appendix 1: Papers Produced by the Wales TUC Research   131
Unit, March 1975–December 1977

Index   132

Illustrations

Illustrations between pages 80 and 81

1. Tom Jones, secretary of the first all-Wales region of the TGWU
2. George Wright at the unofficial inaugural congress at Llandrindod Wells, February 1973
3. Dai Francis (NUM) addressing the 1975 conference from the chair
4. Tony Benn,who gave the Wales TUC £20,000 for research into Welsh economic problems
5. John Morris, Secretary of State for Wales, at the 1975 conference
6. John Jones (Usdaw) addresses the 1976 conference in Welsh
7. Len Murray, general secretary of the TUC 1973–1984
8. Sylvia Jones, the first woman to chair the Wales TUC
9. Michael Foot, leader of the Labour Party and MP for Ebbw Vale, addressing the 1981 Porthcawl conference
10. Emlyn Williams, president of the south Wales area of the NUM during the 1984–1985 miners' strike
11. James Callaghan, Prime Minister and MP for Cardiff South, at the 1977 Tenby conference
12. David Jenkins, general secretary of the Wales TUC, 1983–2004
13. Peter Hain, Secretary of State for Wales and MP for Neath, addresses the Wales TUC conference
14. Felicity Williams, general secretary of the Wales TUC since May 2004

Preface

I first became interested in writing about the Wales TUC when I heard David Jenkins, its general secretary at that time, give a talk in October 1992 at Beddgelert. He spoke about the WTUC's involvement in inward investment and job creation. It was not a trade union activity that would have been unusual in some parts of the world but in Britain it was unique. Moreover, at a time when the TUC and the trade unions generally were the object of an ideological offensive by the government of the day, the Wales TUC and the Welsh Office seemed to be cooperating successfully in this enterprise. I determined to find out more. I was also attracted by the opportunity to write about trade union developments in Wales in the second half of the twentieth century, a neglected topic. Too little attention is paid in studies of industrial relations to regional political economies and patterns of behaviour. In fact, due to pressures of work and other circumstances, much of the research and the writing of the book were delayed until 2003. The delay was fortuitous for it enabled me to take the story through the years of Conservative government and into the challenges raised by the advent of a democratically elected Welsh Assembly.

It is a cliché to write of 'momentous years' but during the thirty years that so far encompass the life of the Wales TUC the Welsh economy has been fundamentally restructured, the governance of Wales put on a completely new footing, economic liberalism has replaced Keynesianism, feminism has increasingly affected social thought and policy, and trade unionism has been pushed from the centre to the margins of political discourse. All these changes are reflected in the narrative that follows. From that narrative three themes emerge.

The first concerns the role of trade unions in contemporary society. They have sustained huge losses in membership and status over the past thirty years, but more than that they have lost the battle of ideas. It is the opponents of trade unionism who have set the agenda for almost a generation. Individualism rather than collectivism is the dominant ethos. Margaret Thatcher put an end to the militant economism that marked British trade unionism in the 1970s and the administration led by Tony Blair shows a marked reluctance to acknowledge that trade unions may have a positive function in society and in today's workplaces. For many people the unions have a male manual worker image redolent of an industrialization that has largely passed away. The challenge facing trade unions is to demonstrate the relevance of their purpose and methods to the workers and employers of today. The major function of the Wales TUC is to act as a pressure group on behalf of trade unions in Wales and their half a million members. But if trade unions are seen as increasingly irrelevant the credibility and authority of the Wales TUC will decline accordingly.

The second theme is the devolution of power and authority. For more than forty years there has been a growth of devolved powers and functions to Wales. Since 1998 administrative devolution has assumed a democratic form, with the Westminster Parliament delegating certain powers and responsibilities to the Welsh Assembly. These may not be as much as some desire but the range of responsibilities is more wide-ranging and significant than many yet understand. The Wales TUC by contrast has less power than some assume. But the Wales TUC was not simply delegated powers from on high. The birth of the Wales TUC is a case study in how to create an organization by confronting a superior body and, by a daring strategy, wrest from it responsibilities it did not wish to surrender. Either way, once responsibilities have been devolved, a change takes place in perceptions of centre and periphery and a persistent tension arises over the issue of resources. For most of its life the Wales TUC has been under-resourced and, despite a post-devolution settlement with the TUC, the issue of resources will not go away. Nor will arguments about the Barnett Formula, which determines how much money goes to the National Assembly. A new dimension will be added to this issue of resource allocation when regions of England gain elected assemblies. Apart from the implications for the Treasury, the desire and capacity of unions to influence decision-making at regional level will raise in acute form the question as to whether the TUC and national trade unions are over-centralized. In Wales and Scotland this question already arises.

These two themes, the role of trade unions today and the consequences of devolution, meet within the third theme – Welsh political culture. This has two dominant characteristics. The first is an attachment to ideas of social justice and equality that have long roots in Welsh history. The second is a sense of Welsh identity that combines pride of country with a conviction that Wales deserves better. The juxtaposition of Edwardian Wales, at the heart of the Royal Navy's imperial dominance, and the searing experience of the inter-war depression is a submerged yet potent folk memory that places an overriding priority upon economic growth and employment. The result is a polity with a left-wing bias but which, behind the banner waving of party politics, has a strong vein of consensualism through a common concern for the condition of Wales. Devolution gives greater freedom to the development of that culture. The genie is out of the bottle and Wales is different from England.

As a consequence of that culture, and unlike the current situation in England, the Wales TUC has been welcomed as a 'social partner' in the achievement of national goals. It is a status that union movements have often desired but ironically it comes when the unions are the weakest they have been for many decades. Social partnership also brings familiar dilemmas. Can the unions rise to the challenge? With what other organizations in civil society can they form alliances? Can they be social partners and retain a campaigning role that establishes their independence, thereby demonstrating that they are partners worth having? The questions have yet to be answered. The future, as ever, remains to be made.

PLAN OF THE BOOK

Chapter 1 sets out the circumstances that led to the emergence of the Wales TUC. So long as mining dominated the Welsh economy there was no need for a Wales TUC. The miners' union and the culture that sprang from it were sufficient. But the decimation of the industry in the 1960s and 1970s, at the same time as employment in manufacturing and services grew, revolutionized the balance of power in the Welsh trade union movement. The NUM was at the forefront of calls for a Wales TUC, but it was increasingly a cry for help. Help came in the shape of the Transport and General Workers' Union and the surprising and critical role played by Jack Jones, its general secretary.

Chapter 2 tells the story of how the Wales TUC became a reality in the face of determined opposition from the TUC. The driving force was George Wright, a trade union leader of a kind not previously known in Wales. It recounts how this Englishman argued the case for Welsh labour, rallied support within Wales through conferences at Llandrindod Wells and Aberystwyth, and raised such a momentum for change that TUC leaders Victor Feather and Len Murray had to concede far more than they wished. The official launch conference at Aberystwyth in 1974 as one of its first deeds voted for an elected Welsh Assembly.

It was fortunate that the birth of the Wales TUC coincided with the election of a Labour government. Chapter 3 explains how with the help of Cabinet ministers – particularly John Morris and Tony Benn – the new organization gained resources and credibility. But, as unemployment grew, so did the Wales TUC's criticisms of the governments of Wilson and Callaghan. The election of Mrs Thatcher and the acceleration of steel closures presented the Wales TUC with a major challenge. The 1980 steel strike opened up differences between the Wales TUC and the TUC, while the government kept its nerve and outfaced the unions. Frustrations in Wales spilled over into talk of civil disobedience.

Mrs Thatcher famously referred to the trade unions as 'the enemy within' and a year-long coal strike ravaged Welsh communities, yet a unique collaboration ensued between the Tory Welsh Office and the Wales TUC. Chapter 4 explains the nature of that collaboration out of which emerged the Wales Co-operative Centre and a highly successful programme of inward investment. The Wales TUC also evolved a system of controlling competition between unions that resulted in the controversial policy of single-union deals. The criticisms and rationale for these policies from a trade union point of view are examined.

Chapter 5 deals with the changing nature of employment and the composition of the working class in Wales in the 1980s and 1990s, and union responses to the precipitous decline in membership. Largely marginalized by the government, the TUC and WTUC gradually found a new industrial relations agenda based upon equal opportunities, racial equality, minimum wage legislation, education and training, women's rights and the concept of partnership. With the Welsh Office increasing its powers throughout this period, the Wales TUC sought more autonomy and greater resources, just when the resources of the unions and the TUC were in decline.

The return of a Labour government brought the Wales TUC in from the cold. The Wales TUC at its inaugural conference in 1974 had called for the early setting up of an elected Legislative Assembly for Wales. It took a leading part in the devolution campaigns of 1978–9 and 1997. Now that the Welsh Assembly Government exists, Chapter 6 discusses its effect upon the role, policies, finances and status of the WTUC. As the voice of organized labour it is recognized as a social partner. But it is one among several. Other partners are better resourced and have louder voices. Is there still a role for a weakened trade union movement? And what are the implications of devolution and regionalization for the TUC and a centralized trade union movement?

Acknowledgements

In writing this brief account of the first thirty years of the Wales TUC I have been helped by a wide range of trade unionists and other interested people. David Jenkins gave unstinted support from the time that I first mentioned my interest in the project, spent many hours discussing it with me, provided access to archive material, but never interfered with my interpretation of events. George Wright welcomed me to his home, discussed at length the development of the Wales TUC and provided invaluable insights into the early years of the organization. John Osmond generously passed to me his collection of original material relating to those early years and Denis Gregory, in addition to discussing his involvement with the Wales TUC, provided copies of research reports written by himself and John Atkinson. Those materials have now been deposited with the National Library at Aberystwyth. Christine Walby loaned me her laptop computer when I was in dire need. Without it I could not have completed the manuscript in time. I was fortunate enough to make contact with Peter O'Brien of the Northern TUC who sent me copies of his publications relating to regionalization and the TUC. Philip Morgan read all the chapters as they were produced and made many valuable comments. Darron Dupre supplied both information and enthusiastic support.

I was also able to draw upon the memories and comments of many who have been involved with the Wales TUC at some time over the past thirty years. Certain of the persons I interviewed prefer to remain anonymous but to them and the following I am most grateful: Julie Cook, Bryn Davies, Jeff Evans, Hywel Francis, Derek Gregory, Noel Hufton, Clare Jenkins, Jack Jones, John Jones, Keith Jones, Simon Jones, John Monks, Jim Morris, Ian Spence, Jim Ryan, Lyn Tregonning, Hywel Vaughan, Felicity Williams. I am grateful to the staff of the Clwyd Record Office, Swansea University Library, the South Wales Miners' Library, Swansea, the National Library of Wales, the Modern Records Centre at Warwick University and Glynneath Public Library for their kind assistance. My former employer, Coleg Harlech, granted me study leave in the autumn of 1994 to begin this project and the Business School at the University of Wales, Cardiff, granted me research facilities as a Visiting Scholar at that time. I am indebted to them both. My greatest debt is to my wife Joan who single-handedly refurbished a house while I was writing but found time to read, and correct, the manuscript. All errors remaining are mine.

Abbreviations

ACAS	Advisory, Conciliation and Arbitration Service
AEEU	Amalgamated Engineering and Electrical Union (merger of AEU and EETPU; see AMICUS)
AEU	Amalgamated Engineering Union
AMICUS	Union formed by the merger of AEEU and MSF
APEX	Association of Professional, Executive, Clerical and Computer Staff (now merged with GMB)
ASTMS	Association of Scientific, Technical and Managerial Staff
AUEW	Amalgamated Union of Engineering Workers (later the AEU)
BSC	British Steel Corporation
CAWU	Clerical and Administrative Workers' Union (later APEX)
CBI	Confederation of British Industry
COHSE	Confederation of Health Service Employees (see Unison)
CP	Communist Party
CWU	Communication Workers' Union
DBRW	Development Board for Rural Wales
EEC	European Economic Community
EETPU	Electrical, Electronic, Telecommunications and Plumbing Union
EOC	Equal Opportunities Commission
EU	European Union
GMB	General, Municipal and Boilermakers' Union
GMWU	General and Municipal Workers' Union
GPMU	Graphical, Paper and Media Union
IRSF	Inland Revenue Staff Association
ISTC	Iron and Steel Trades Confederation
MSC	Manpower Services Commission
MSF	Manufacturing, Science, Finance (a merger of ASTMS and TASS)
NALGO	National and Local Government Officers' Association (see Unison)
NASUWT	National Association of Schoolmasters/Union of Women Teachers

NATFHE	National Association of Teachers in Further and Higher Education
NCB	National Coal Board
NEB	National Enterprise Board
NEDC	National Economic Development Council
NUGMW	National Union of General and Municipal Workers (now GMB)
NUM	National Union of Mineworkers
NUPE	National Union of Public Service Employees (see Unison)
NUR	National Union of Railwaymen
NUT	National Union of Teachers
PCS	Public and Commercial Services Union
RAC	Regional Advisory Council of the TUC
RMT	National Union of Rail, Maritime and Transport Workers
SOGAT82	Society of Graphical and Allied Trades
TASS	Technical, Administrative and Supervisory Staffs
TEC	Training and Enterprise Council
TGWU	Transport and General Workers' Union
TUC	Trades Union Congress
TURU	Trade Union Research Unit
UCATT	Union of Construction, Allied Trades and Technicians
Unison	Formed in 1993 through amalgamation of COHSE, NALGO and NUPE
USDAW	Union of Shop, Distributive and Allied Workers
WAG	Welsh Assembly Government
WDA	Welsh Development Agency
WTUC	Wales Trade Union Council
WULF	Wales Union Learning Fund

Chapter 1

All Change

The sixties was a swinging decade – and in Wales some of us were swinging to the music of a nation reborn.

(John Davies)

It is well known that change is the only constant, but for Wales in the 1960s all aspects of its economic, social and political life were in flux. The optimism about the economy that marked the early years of the decade – Brinley Thomas's 1962 volume[1] was subtitled *Studies in Expansion* – had given way by 1968 to severe misgivings. In politics, thirteen years of Conservative rule yielded in 1964 to Labour administrations with strong Welsh associations, yet increasing numbers of electors voted for Plaid Cymru and by 1970 the Conservatives were back in office. The ending of national service in 1960, rising incomes and the waning influence of religion resulted in a decline of deference, a rise in consumerism and the creation of a youth culture that cut across social classes. Some of the younger generation put their energy into a militant Welsh–language crusade, the majority into rock and roll. Most voted for the Sunday opening of pubs. A new Wales was in the making.

Helping to shape that new Wales were institutions created out of a combination of administrative devolution and cultural nationalism: the Welsh Office in 1964, the Welsh Arts Council and a Language Act in 1967, the Wales Tourist Board in 1969, the Sports Council for Wales in 1971, the Land Authority for Wales in 1975, the Welsh Development Agency in 1976 and the Development Board for Rural Wales in 1977. The tide of institutional devolution was therefore in full flood when the Wales TUC began its official existence in 1974. It took its place, apparently, alongside those other institutions. Such a view is understandable but mistaken.

The Wales TUC is neither a quango nor a government department. It is an independent democratically elected pressure group. Its purpose is to represent the trade unions and workers of Wales. Consequently, the reasons for its existence and purpose cannot be found in party-political moves to devolution, or in Whitehall's reluctant acquiescence in decentralization. It emerged when trade union power was at its post-war zenith in Britain, when the modernization of the Welsh economy was well on the way to creating a new working class, but when the Keynesian consensus on how to run the economy was breaking down and when fears were mounting about the future for jobs in Wales. The time was ripe for a new body to express the hopes and fears of Welsh workers and the political climate in the 1960s, with its new emphasis upon a separate Welsh identity, was conducive to its appearance. But the decision to create such a body required much more than Welsh sentiment. It required the will and the resources to confront the power of the British Trades Union Congress, *the* TUC.

The TUC, founded in 1868, is the oldest national, independent trade union organization in the world. Through the trade unions affiliated to it, the TUC represents over 95 per cent of the organized workers in the United Kingdom and speaks for them in a variety of national and international forums. Although many trade unions affiliate to the Labour Party, the TUC has never done so and consequently contains within its ranks a number of unions that do not affiliate to Labour or any other party. In the 1960s its general secretary was George Woodcock, an aloof and cynical man with a first-class brain, whose bushy eyebrows and frequent appearances on television made him a household name. His successor from March 1969 to September 1973 was Victor (Vic) Feather, a gregarious Yorkshire man, tough negotiator and uncompromising anti-communist. Both served the TUC for over thirty years and neither could conceive of any dilution in its authority, and in the 1960s and 1970s that authority was at its peacetime height.

It is one of the ironies of the various attempts by the state to curb trade union power that it only succeeded in enhancing the status of the TUC. When it was founded in 1868, the TUC was intended to be, and remains, a forum in which affiliated unions pursue their joint interests. But it is not an institution to which they have given significant resources or power. Nonetheless, state intervention in industrial relations in the 1960s and 1970s had a significant impact upon its internal authority *vis-à-vis* its affiliates and boosted its external authority in relations with employers' associations and the government.

When from 1961 governments desired the union viewpoint on economic planning, incomes policy or labour legislation they turned to the TUC. Consequently, many unions that had remained aloof from the

TUC, particularly those organizing professional workers, affiliated in order to have their voice heard. In addition to unions representing university teachers and middle and senior grade civil servants, the two largest white-collar unions at that time joined: the National and Local Government Officers' Association (NALGO) in 1964 and the National Union of Teachers (NUT) in 1970. Meanwhile, overall trade union membership continued to rise: from 9.8 million in 1960 to 13 million by 1978. The TUC gained authority too from its stand against the Industrial Relations Act 1971. Besides demonstrating its ability to frustrate that legislation, it exercised a notable degree of discipline over its affiliates at that time. Government initiatives such as the National Economic Development Council (NEDC) or the National Enterprise Board (NEB) also had an impact upon the internal organization of the TUC. It developed its industry committees, expanded its provision for trade union training and education, and from 1968 published its distinctive annual economic reviews.[2]

But it had a weakness. In England and Wales it had a system of Regional Advisory Councils (RACs) that were descendants of emergency wartime arrangements. These RACs were empowered to 'act as the agent of the Trades Union Congress' under the direction of the General Council of the TUC. They could nominate union representatives on to government boards and committees at regional level, and 'were encouraged to take an active interest in policy issues relating to production, employment, education and social insurance'. The members of these regional committees were invariably full-time union officials in each region, with the chairman and deputy chairman chosen by the General Council. This enabled the TUC leadership 'to exert a controlling influence on union–government relations below the national level'.[3] It was a control that they had difficulty in asserting over trades councils despite a system of registering TUC recognized councils and an annual conference organized by the TUC. Trades councils linked together branches of different unions in a town or geographical area, providing a meeting place for ordinary members and a framework for political activity and local campaigns. In Wales in the late 1960s there were two Regional Advisory Councils, one for the north and one for the south, and around fifty trades councils organized in four area federations.

Both the advisory committees and the trades councils had grown in an *ad hoc* fashion, and neither could claim to be the single authoritative voice of the trade union movement in the regions – a fact that in the best of times gave rise to tensions between them. There was also a history of uneasy relations between the TUC and the trades councils. Although the TUC valued them as a direct channel to grass-root opinion on a variety of issues, it was often unhappy with the answers it received. Trades council members tended to have more radical opinions than those held by the TUC secretariat. Vic Feather spent considerable time and effort in the 1950s investigating Communist Party influence in the trades councils.[4] But from the late 1950s there was a new and growing factor that exacerbated the divide between the RACs, composed almost entirely of full-time officials, and the rank and file in the trades councils. This was the increasing number of trade union activists elected at factory level to represent their fellow workers, the 'shop stewards'. In Wales it was linked to far-reaching changes in its post-war industrial structure. One incident illustrates how these two strands were entwined.

WORKPLACE UNIONISM

On Tuesday morning, 6 April 1971, 1,600 workers from the Ford Motor Company factory at Swansea crowded into the Windsor Cinema, Neath, for a mass meeting. For almost ten weeks the 50,000 employees of the Ford Motor Company in Britain had been on strike, arguing for parity of earnings with car workers in Coventry. Now, in response to a company offer, all other plants in the Ford empire had returned to work except those at Halewood (Liverpool) and Swansea – both had been the first to come out on strike (unofficially) and both still refused to accept the settlement agreed a week earlier between the company and the trade union negotiators. In Neath that day to persuade them to return to work was Moss Evans, engineering national officer of the Transport and General Workers' Union (TGWU), a Welshman whose trade union career had been forged in the car factories of the West Midlands. After two-and-a-quarter hours the strikers voted overwhelmingly by a show of hands for a return to work. The next day Evans achieved the same result at Halewood: the strike was over. The agreement was for a 33 per cent wage increase over two years.[5] The Heath government, which a few days earlier had wound up the National Board for Prices and Incomes, expressed its dislike of the agreement but Vauxhall Motors and British Leyland offered similar deals in the same month.

By 1971 such strikes were common in Britain. Car workers were seen as the most aggressive section of the British working class; comparisons of pay levels between different factories in the same industry or between different grades of workers in the same plant were a common cause of disputes; and the TGWU, with 1.6 million members and a General Secretary, Jack Jones, who strongly promoted shop steward power, was setting the pace in achieving substantial gains for its members. The post-war achievement of 'a high and stable level of employment' in line with the pledge in the famous 1944 White Paper on Employment Policy had strengthened workers' bargaining power and they did not hesitate to exercise it where they could. Decisions over pay and then over working arrangements, overtime and manning, discipline and redundancy, became more and more matters to be settled in each factory or workplace between shop stewards and local managers rather than subjects for national bargaining. Estimates of the number of shop stewards vary, but a careful assessment suggests that there were 175,000 in the United Kingdom in 1966 and by 1978 they were thought to number over 250,000.[6]

Workplace bargaining frequently took the form of a jostling for advantage between different groups of workers to achieve short-term gains by disorderly, even disruptive means. There was a sharp increase in the number of strikes, many of them unofficial. Excluding the coal industry (a special case), strikes more than trebled between 1960 and 1970 – from 1,166 to 3,746. From the early 1960s 'the trade union question' became the dominant issue in British domestic politics and the state began to introduce a wide range of reforms into the industrial relations system. The net result, as noted earlier, was an increase in the influence of the TUC.

The involvement of the Swansea workers in the 1971 national Ford strike illustrates a number of the themes briefly mentioned above: the strength of workplace organization and a preparedness to take unofficial strike action; a refusal to fall into line with official union policy until those on strike had debated it face to face with the union's chief negotiator ('They played hell with me'[7]); a preference for resolving issues by show of hands in a mass meeting rather than by secret ballot; and a determin-ation to 'catch up' with workers in comparable situations. But it also illustrates the post-war rebuilding of the Welsh economy. Ford was just one of a number of multi-national corporations that had sited plants in Wales, many of them in the booming consumer durable industries.

RECONSTRUCTING WALES

Old industrial Wales had been built upon coal and slate, iron and steel. The products of furnace and mine depended upon wage labour carried out almost entirely by men in dirty, difficult and dangerous conditions. In the early decades of the twentieth century a quarter of all those employed in Wales worked in the mines and quarries. In 1930 some 76 per cent of the insured population of Glamorgan worked in the coal, steel and tinplate industries. Around each pit or steelworks were communities usually small in scale, almost entirely working class, Nonconformist in religious affiliation, and characterized by a culture that encompassed neighbourliness, self-confidence and profound democratic instincts. By the end of the Great War trade unionism was firmly established in the steel and tinplate industries, on the docks and on the railways, in slate quarrying and overwhelmingly in coalmining where the South Wales Miners' Federation was a major cultural as well as industrial force. But links with the rest of the British economy were limited. The products of Welsh industry went around the world rather than across Offa's Dyke. The loss of export markets after 1921, and the inter-war depression that followed, savagely wounded that pre-war self-confidence and decimated trade union membership.

The fact was that the industrial structure of Wales had remained in its nineteenth-century mould until it decayed in the 1920s and 1930s. The massive unemployment of the depression years was seen to be the result of 'having too many eggs in one basket' and the answer was firmly believed to be a diversification of employment by bringing in new industries and this was carried through in ways that have been well documented.[8] The task was not to be left to market forces. It required deliberate state action and the post-war Labour government set about it with a will. By the vigorous use of the Distribution of Industry Act, 1945, it steered expanding firms away from the Midlands and the south-east of England and into the 'development areas', which included large parts of north and south Wales. The wartime ordnance factories at Hirwaun, Bridgend and Pembrey were transformed into trading estates, similar to the one set up at Treforest in 1936, and another added at Fforestfach near Swansea. In addition, over 400 new industrial buildings were put up in Wales between 1945 and 1952. There followed an influx of major employers and the further development of existing factories. Hoover went to Merthyr Tydfil, Dunlop-Semtex to Brynmawr, Enfield Clocks to Ystradgynlais, ICI Nylon Spinners to Pontypool and the factories producing electrical switchgear at Blackwood and cables at Aberdare expanded. By the early 1950s unemployment in Wales was consistently below 3 per cent. A recession in 1958–9, combined with defence cuts and the accelerated closure of the old tinplate, sheet and steelworks, stimulated a burst of activity by the Macmillan government. A £2 million factory was erected at Swansea for the ill-fated Prestcold refrigerator project. Revlon cosmetics came to Maesteg, Hotpoint to Llandudno. The motorcar industry was pressurized to invest in Wales and the Rover Company came to Cardiff, Fisher and Ludlow to Llanelli where the Morris Motors factory was expanding, and Ferodo and Bernard Wardle to Caernarfon.

A third phase of vigorous government intervention began in 1965 after the return of a Labour government in 1964 (Harold Wilson gave the campaign keynote speech on economic policy at Swansea). Once again a number of important firms came to Wales, including Johnson and Johnson to Pontllanfraith, Morganite Carbon to Swansea, and Jefferson Chemicals to Llanelli. The car industry increased its stake in Wales. Ford moved into the abandoned Prestcold factory and gave employment to almost 2,000, making axles and gearboxes. The Borg–Warner automatic transmission company went to Kenfig Hill, Austin–Crompton Parkinson to Tredegar, Girlings set up a major car component factory at Cwmbran. By 1970 manufacturing had grown to employ over 200,000 workers in south Wales, more than coal and steel combined.

The result was that Welsh trade unionism shared the characteristics of the new unionism of the 1960s. Large workplaces, employing 500–3,000 people, encouraged unionization and shop steward organization.[9] A number of factories were branches of international companies and concentrated upon assembly-line processes that required predominantly semi-skilled and unskilled labour. The customs and practices of coal and steel were replaced by more fragmented work practices, by a more intensive pace of work and closer supervision. There was little intrinsic satisfaction in the work. With trading estates and factories predominantly on the periphery of the coalfield, many employees faced daily journeys to work. To that extent there was a loss of the networks that strengthened class identity in the traditional coal and steel communities, where work, home and union branch coexisted. Twenty years of economic growth and increasing affluence had dissipated the 'depression mentality', particularly among the younger generation, and union membership was less a class statement than an expression of instrumental collectivism, a vehicle on the road to higher earnings. In these respects Welsh workers were little different from their English counterparts and, like them, they swelled the membership of the unions that organized Britain's factory workers – the general unions, the vehicle builders, the engineers and electricians. In firms where there was multi-plant bargaining, as in Ford, ICI, Dunlop, Metal Box and Hoover, shop stewards from Wales were part of shop steward combine committees that exchanged information and planned their next wage claims. In a wide range of craft unions in engineering and building, and in the TGWU, Welsh shop stewards sat on local, regional and national decision-making bodies. They held office in their local trades councils. But the north and south Wales advisory committees of the TUC – enclaves of full-time officers – remained closed to them. It was a situation waiting for reform.

The 1960s began in a mood of optimism that later evaporated. 'The redevelopment of South Wales has been one of the great success stories of the past thirty years', commented a *Times* leader in March 1963. Massive investments in modern steel plants had brought prosperity. The largest steelworks in Britain was the Abbey works at Margam, Port Talbot, with its associated tinplate plants at Trostre and Velindre. With further post-war investments at Ebbw Vale, East Moors Cardiff and Shotton, the Welsh steel industry at the beginning of the 1960s was providing over a quarter of the steel produced in Britain. In 1962 the great steelworks at Llanwern went into production. By 1963 Wales was producing all of the UK's tinplate, and almost the entire UK output of sheet steel – the basic material for the vehicle and consumer durable industries. In 1965, the major steelworks in Wales were employing 70,650 workers and were the major factor in driving forward the Welsh economy.

Llanwern works was called Eldorado. Port Talbot was known as Treasure Island; the local branch of the Trustee Savings Bank was nicknamed The Rowing Club – 'the company puts our pay in there on a Thursday, and by lunch-time we've taken it out again. It's a case of in–out, in–out' – and the huge workingmen's clubs were reputed to have bar takings of well over £100,000 a year. 'South Wales likes to spend. It has never had money before. It has waited a long time. It is determined to enjoy.'[10]

Optimism was not based upon the steel industry alone. It was enhanced by the arrival of high-technology industries that seemed to promise a new and modern Wales. Milford Haven became the largest oil port in Britain as a succession of companies opened large refineries – Esso in 1960, BP in 1961, Texaco in 1964, Gulf Oil in 1968, Amoco in 1973. Nuclear power stations were built at Trawsfynydd and at Wylfa Head on Anglesey. Major petro-chemical and plastics plants were established at Barry and Baglan Bay. White-collar civil service jobs became high profile.

The Welsh Office kept expanding. The Driving Vehicle Licence Centre came to Swansea as part of a policy of bringing government jobs to Wales. An office to administer investment grants went to Cardiff, as did offices for the Land Commission and the Inland Revenue. A new Passport Office went to Newport, and the Royal Mint was transferred from London to Llantrisant. There were visible changes to the communications infrastructure. Government investment in the road network increased mobility within the country and, via the Severn Bridge and the M4, the three-lane heads of the valleys road (A465) between Hirwaun and Abergavenny and the M50, Welsh steel products found it easier to reach their markets in the Midlands. In the north improvements to the A55 opened up links to Merseyside. By 1965, 48 per cent of Welsh employees were engaged in services and by 1974 the majority of Welsh workers were working in health, education, public administration, transport and communications, retailing, hotels and catering.

Yet fears about the economic future were never far away. Branch factories were regarded, with reason, as susceptible to closure when the general economy faltered. The implementation of the 1963 Beeching Report cost jobs as well as hundreds of miles of railway track. Above all, it was becoming clear that all the post-war efforts to rebuild the economy would not be sufficient to make up for the loss of jobs in coal and the gathering redundancies in steel. The affluence that surrounded the steelworks was built on shaky foundations. Technological change, and increasing competition in a slowly growing world market from low-cost steelworks in Japan, Italy and the USA, pointed to the need for further technical innovation and the raising of productivity. As early as May 1964 the Steel Company of Wales at Port Talbot hired Emerson Consultants to examine its organization and in particular its wages structure and manning. At that time over 17,000 people were employed on the Margam site.[11] The estimates of overmanning that emerged ranged from 6,000 to 9,000 men. The problems were not confined to Port Talbot. In 1973 plans were published to reduce the numbers employed at Shotton by 6,000, at Ebbw Vale by 4,500, and Cardiff by 4,100. The redundancies in steel were to become the focus of a major campaign by the Wales TUC.

More serious, and more immediate, was the reality of pit closures with large-scale unemployment. The post-war reconstruction of coal under nationalization, with the closure of worked out and inefficient pits, had resulted by 1959 in a contraction to 141 mines employing 93,000 in south Wales. In the next ten years, demand for coal declined rapidly in the face of competition from cleaner and cheaper fuels. The result was more and more closures and a devastating rundown in manpower. By 1973 there were just fifty-three pits employing 35,000. No working collieries remained in the Afan and Swansea valleys, just two were working in the Rhondda (in 1947 there had been twenty-five) and all over the South Wales Coalfield towns and villages found that their original *raison d'être* had disappeared. Similar closures took place in north Wales. Mining had become a relatively small part of the economy.[12] Over 40 per cent of the mining labour force had been thrown on the job market. Kenneth Morgan estimates: 'No less than 60,000 jobs disappeared between 1964 and 1970 alone, and perhaps 100,000 or more in the entire period 1964 to 1976'. Unemployment in Wales rose from 2.9 per cent in 1966 to 4.7 per cent in 1972.[13]

THE ROAD TO 1972

With these problems growing, it was clear that a forum was required in which the issues could be debated by the trade union movement and a common policy agreed for presentation to the new Welsh Office. Separate Trades Union Congresses existed for Ireland and Scotland and there was a long history of calls for a separate Wales TUC along the lines of the Scottish and Irish bodies. The North Wales Quarrymen's Union held a seat on the TUC General Council for many years and argued more than once that there should be a separate body for Wales. The tinplate section of the Dock, Wharf and Riverside Workers' Union is said to have made such a proposition in 1919. Plaid Cymru published a pamphlet on that theme in the mid-1940s and the Communist Party between 1938 and 1948 issued twenty pamphlets on a range of devolutionary measures.[14] Throughout the 1940s and 1950s various trade union bodies in Wales pursued the idea, largely influenced by a nationalist or communist point of view. In December 1943 delegates in the anthracite area of the South Wales Miners' Federation passed a resolution calling for a separate TUC for Wales. The Cardiff Trades Council did the same in 1947. The Pontardulais branch of the Electrical Trades Union passed a similar resolution in 1954, and in 1961, 1964 and 1965 branches of the Amalgamated Union of Foundry Workers expressed support. But by the mid-1960s ideology was joined by pragmatism. It is true that the greatest pressure continued to come from the left – the federations of trades councils and the south Wales area of the National Union of Mineworkers – but the problems were real, the need more urgent.

From 1966 the calls became persistent. In January of that year the south Wales RAC, in response to the foundry workers, decided to contact its north Wales counterpart to ascertain its views. Also in January the three federations of trades councils in south Wales, at a joint conference, passed a resolution calling for a Welsh TUC, as did the Llanelli trades council. In May the annual conference of the NUM south Wales area supported 'the growing demand for a TUC to be set up for Wales'.[15] By then the north Wales RAC had rejected the idea. 'Our main objection was that it was impractical to organise as Wales is just not an economic unit. Trade unions and industries in North and South Wales are totally different and have completely different problems.' Both the unions and major companies in the north had close affiliations with Merseyside. It was also pointed out that:

> there would be no purpose in pursuing the matter further because it would rest finally with the Unions, particularly as they would have to agree to pay an additional affiliation fee per member in order to finance and establish a Welsh TUC if it were set up.[16]

At the annual meeting of the north Wales RAC on 3 February 1967 the secretary, Tom Jones, commented that it would be 'silly to set up a costly ornament'. But the issue would not go away. In March 1968 the Glamorgan federation of trades councils sought a meeting with the south Wales RAC to discuss closer liaison and the formation of a Welsh TUC. The meeting was held in May when D. Ivor Davies put the federation's case, was thanked for his pains, and told that the RAC would respond in due course.

At first it appeared that progress would be made. Graham Saunders, full-time officer of the Clerical and Administrative Workers' Union in south Wales, and secretary of the south Wales RAC, told the *Western Mail* (4 June 1968), 'We feel the time has come when the interests of all Welsh workers could be best served by such a congress.' But this time the pressure had been felt in London and George Woodcock expressed his view: 'A Welsh TUC would only arise if there was a Welsh government and a Welsh Confederation of Employers.'[17] At a meeting in July at Newtown the chairmen and secretaries of the north and south RACs came to the conclusion that progress would depend upon unions with members in Wales forming themselves into one unit for the whole of Wales, which was not at all the current position. There was also the issue of the cost to unions of affiliating to such an organization.

With the prospect of a Welsh TUC once again rejected there was still the issue of closer working between the trades council federations and the south Wales RAC. The executives of the north and south RACs, together with representatives of the south Wales federations, met in Llandrindod Wells on 7 May 1969, where it was agreed that RAC officers and federation officers should meet quarterly. The two RACs also agreed to set up a joint executive and, whilst continuing to act independently on matters reflecting their respective areas, to act jointly on matters affecting Wales as a whole. This latter decision was surely promoted by Tom Jones, the north Wales secretary, who had changed his mind about the need for a Wales TUC and who saw the measure as a half-way house towards that destination. Neither proposal got off the ground, principally because the south Wales RAC was a reluctant participant. As D. Ivor Davies, secretary of the Glamorgan Trades Council Federation, told the annual meeting of the TUC held in Brighton in 1970:

> the Glamorgan Federation of Trades Councils has been trying for twelve years to establish a close relationship with the South Wales Regional Advisory Committee, and if we were lepers we could not have been more excluded from any deliberations or discussions with that body.[18]

It was clear to him, as to others, that the full-time officials who sat on the RACs 'were not really grappling with the problems of Wales. They wanted to concentrate on the problems of their own unions.'[19] In these circumstances, and with Wales on the way to acquiring a variety of devolved institutions, calls for a Wales TUC were not going to disappear.

The idea was put forward again in 1970 by the south Wales NUM following a resolution by the Merthyr Vale lodge. Once again there was no progress. At the annual meeting of the south Wales RAC in November 1971 Dai Francis moved a motion on behalf of the NUM: 'The South Wales Area requests the TUC Advisory Committee to convene a special meeting of Trade Unions in South Wales with the view of forming a Welsh Trade Union Congress.' It was seconded by Les Paul a lay member of the executive of the Inland Revenue Staff Association and one of the few lay members on the RAC. The motion was defeated by a majority of full-time union officials.[20] There is no escaping the impression that, after Ron Mathias resigned the secretaryship in August 1967, upon his appointment as a full-time member of the National Board for Prices and Incomes, the south Wales RAC became an increasingly inward-looking body without the capacity to appraise the social and economic changes taking place all around it or even to rise above petty self-interest. Throughout the negotiations that led to the setting up of the Wales TUC the south Wales RAC was a persistent opponent of the project.

But the key piece in the jigsaw had already been put in place in July 1968 in the unlikely setting of Belfast. The Rules Revision Conference of the TGWU meeting in that city had made a number of sweeping changes to the union's constitution, initiated by Jack Jones the heir-apparent to Frank Cousins as general secretary. One of them, largely disregarded within the union and outside Wales, was the amalgamation of regions 4 and 13 to create a new all-Wales region of the union. This was more than a simple administrative tidying up. Jones, who was to become the 'most formidable, intellectually fertile and effective leader since Ernest Bevin'[21] had a vision for the union and for the trade union movement as a whole. It was based on the devolution of power. A passionate believer that democracy was a good to be pursued generally, he introduced a series of reforms based upon giving more information and power to ordinary workers. He wanted workers and their shopfloor representatives to share in the decisions affecting their future and to participate in industrial progress.[22] The formation of a single Wales region was a deliberate move towards the setting up of a Wales TUC in line with these beliefs. 'There were the examples of the Scottish and Irish TUCs and I did not see that Wales should be any different'.[23]

The regional secretary of the new all-Wales region would be 61-year-old Tom Jones, secretary of the TGWU's north Wales region since 1953, and secretary of the north Wales RAC. Between Tom Jones and Jack Jones there was a mutual respect. Both had fought on the Republican side in the Spanish Civil War, and both had been wounded in the cause. 'Taking Tom from the north and putting him in charge of the whole region was a hard decision because of reservations in south Wales about northerners. But Tom was the only possible candidate.'[24] Moreover, Tom Jones, from his experience as a member of the Welsh Economic Council and observation of pressures upon the RACs, recognized the validity of Jack Jones's vision for Wales. 'For too long the hills have divided us – now we must be united', he told the *Western Mail* on 4 June 1968. But Tom was too old to take on the task, particularly as welding the two TGWU regions together was not straightforward. Some officers were concerned that it would affect their promotion prospects, branch officials were wary of losing their positions on main union committees. There were the long-standing rivalries between north and south. The affairs of the region came first.

The moment of change came in 1972. It began with the first national miners' strike since 1926. No union had been affected more by the industrial restructuring of Wales than the NUM. From the last quarter of the nineteenth century until the 1960s coalmining had created a distinctive society that encompassed most of the population. The daily experience of life underground was 'so powerful that it was a central formative influence' binding men and communities together.[25] To speak of the Welsh working class was to speak of the miners. Their union, the South Wales Miners' Federation renamed from 1 January 1945 as the South Wales Area of the NUM, was an organic part of daily life in the community, their collective solidarity as strong in defeat as in victory. But almost 200,000 had left the industry since 1913. Collieries had become isolated pockets of employment. The leadership that lodge officials had held in industrial and political life for over sixty years was now largely lost. No longer could people turn to their local NUM lodge officials for help and advice. The funds for the coal industry welfare schemes, supporting the Miners' Institutes and Welfare Halls that for generations had served as libraries, and more recently as cinemas, dried up. Constituency Labour parties formerly dominated by NUM delegates now came under other influences. In 1945 there had been thirteen NUM-sponsored MPs in south Wales, by 1974 there were none. The social, industrial and political power of the NUM was visibly ebbing away.

Yet the successful strike of 1972 seemed to suggest that, despite pit closures and membership decline, the NUM was still a force to be reckoned with. Indeed it was, as would be shown again two years later. But they were not victories won by the miners alone. The critical event in 1972 was the siege of the Saltley Marsh Coal Depot in Birmingham, when on 10 February almost 40,000 workers in Birmingham factories downed tools in support of the miners, and 10,000 marched to Saltley to join the 2,000 miners already there. Throughout the dispute dockers and lorry drivers – both members of the TGWU – refused to unload coal imports or move oil supplies. Jack Jones had pledged that picket lines would not be crossed and that his members would assist the miners in any way they could. The strike came at the height of trade union hostility to the Industrial Relations Act 1971 and to the Heath government's attempt to rein in public service pay awards. There was universal determination in the labour movement that the miners would not be defeated.

Even so, there were problems in Wales. From the Midlands region of the TGWU two senior officials were told to give assistance; they were Alan Law, the Birmingham district officer for road haulage, a meticulous and determined union organizer who had been at Saltley, and George Wright, the regional secretary for the engineering and car industries – a position formerly held by Jack Jones and Moss Evans – and one of the fast-rising stars of the union.[26] Wright visited Dai Francis, the secretary of the south Wales NUM, and found him deeply concerned that members of the Clerical and Administrative Workers' Union (CAWU), despite TUC guidelines, had been involved in angry scenes with NUM pickets and that on at least one occasion (19 January) 400 had crossed picket lines at the Ystradmynach NCB Area Office. Moreover, Graham Saunders, the full-time officer responsible for the CAWU in south Wales was also the secretary of the TUC's south Wales RAC. It was evident to Wright and Francis that trade union solidarity was not what it should be, and a shake-up had to take place.[27] In May 1972 the south Wales miners again called for a Wales TUC to be discussed at the RAC annual meeting in November. It was not.

The situation was now coming to a head. Although the miners had humiliated the Heath government they could not stop pit closures; in steel, forecasts of severe job losses were being openly discussed. At a time of heightened national identity it was evident that a vacuum existed at the heart of the Welsh trade union movement. An act of leadership was needed. Once again, the key moves were made by Jack Jones.

With Tom Jones approaching sixty-five it was time to decide who should be his successor. Jack Jones recalled,

> When the time came, a candidate was sought within Wales but there was no one of that capacity there. Regional Secretary is an important job. After that it was thrown open to the whole of the union and it came down to two – George and a man from Scotland.[28]

George Wright arrived in Wales on 22 July 1972 as regional secretary designate.

The stage was now set for the final move. At the Labour Party Conference in the first week of October Jack Jones discussed the issue of a Wales TUC with Tom Jones and on his return to Wales Tom wrote to Dai Francis on 9 October:

> As you will know there has been a desire amongst a substantial body of trade unionists in Wales for some time that a Democratic Trades Union Congress be formed in place of the two Regional Advisory Committees of the British TUC which are made up of full time Union Officers . . .

At the Labour Party Conference in Blackpool last week I had a long chat with Brother Jack Jones our General Secretary about a Welsh TUC and he has authorised me to agree to the general principle of setting up such an Organisation.

Political and economic events in Wales, Britain and Europe are moving rapidly and it behoves us to prepare for the coming changes by strengthening and welding together the foundations of a strong Democratic Trade Union movement in Wales. I am certain your Union would readily agree with this idea.

I would be glad therefore if your Executive Council in South Wales would agree to meet our Welsh Regional Committee at a convenient date in our Hall in Cardiff to discuss the principle of a Democratic Welsh Trades Union Congress.

There is little doubt that this was no more than a formal confirmation of a telephone conversation that they had already had, for on the same day the *Western Mail* carried the headline: 'Plan to set up a Welsh TUC' and quoted Tom Jones as saying that a Welsh TUC would be able to look after the economic interests of the Principality. In conversation with Dai Francis Tom Jones had gone as far as to say that, even if they did not get the support of other unions, the TGWU and the NUM could 'go it alone'. Dai Francis, records Jones, 'was taken aback'[29] by the boldness of the decision. The task of delivering it was given to George Wright.

Chapter 2

The Confrontation

A good agreement is one that both sides can live with. (George Wright)

The Wales TUC was born out of confrontation. For almost a year before its final form was settled the TUC had argued against its necessity, its constitution and intentions, and even against its name. And when, after more than twenty years of grass-roots pressure, the leaders of the two most prominent unions in Wales unilaterally declared in October 1972 that they were going to form a Welsh Trades Union Congress, it was driven through to inauguration by an Englishman newly arrived in Wales, backed by the most powerful trade union leader on the TUC general council. Even then, in a classic trade union compromise, it emerged less than it seemed but more than it might have been.

When Tom Jones made that unilateral declaration he and Dai Francis were playing a strong hand. The TGWU was the largest union in Wales and the NUM had just emerged from a successful national strike and was seen to be, once again, in the vanguard of the Welsh working class. Tom Jones knew he had the backing of his general secretary and consequently of TGWU executive committees in Wales and in London and Dai Francis knew that the declaration would be welcomed by rank-and-file trade unionists in the trades councils and miners' lodges. But they knew too that there would be opposition from within Wales and from outside. Some members of the Labour Party's regional council initially regarded it with suspicion. The Communist Party was known to favour a Wales TUC and Dai Francis was a member of the CP, while Tom Jones was always remembered as a member of the International Brigade, rather than as the TGWU's north Wales regional secretary appointed by the rabidly anti-communist Arthur Deakin. Moreover, he was a north Walian, a fact that in itself aroused antipathy in some. In truth, these were petty objections from lesser men. Tom Jones was a straight talking no-nonsense negotiator who carried about him the aura of a man who had fought as a machine-gunner and survived a death sentence in a Spanish fascist prison. Dai Francis was a tough negotiator and a communist. He was also a man with a gift for friendship, a lover of music and poetry who in 1974 was made a member of the Gorsedd of Bards of the National Eisteddfod. In Wright's words 'a chapel communist', he transcended sectarian boundaries.[1] They were a formidable combination but Jones was in his retirement year and Francis was past sixty and facing more pit closures and a falling membership. They had fired the first shot but from then on the battle was largely in George Wright's hands. The opposition that really mattered to their announcement would come from the TUC in London.

GEORGE WRIGHT

George Wright was the kind of full-time trade union official who had not been seen in Wales before. It was not that he was English, or that he was young – at thirty-six the youngest regional secretary designate in the TGWU. It was that he had learned his trade unionism in the heartland of post-war workplace organization, the car industry of the West Midlands, a formidable school. The middle child of nine he started work at the Austin Longbridge car plant in Birmingham when he was nineteen; at twenty he was on the picket line amidst the violent scenes of 1956 and met Jack Jones, the recently appointed regional secretary;[2] and at twenty-two he was the leading shop steward for the Mini engine and gearbox section. In the 1960s the proportion of the workers' pay packet determined by workplace bargaining was higher in the vehicle industry than in any other, and no other region had such a concentration of workplace bargainers as the TGWU's region 5 (Midlands). It was there that Jack Jones and his *confidant* Harry Urwin pursued a policy of devolving power to lay members and their shopfloor representatives, a policy they later promoted within the union as a whole when they rose to national office.[3] Moss Evans, Jones's successor, was nurtured in that culture, and so was George Wright. He honed his bargaining skills as piecework negotiator in the Longbridge paint shop before moving to the Mini project. 'I had a good head for figures but there's more to negotiating than that. I knew how to persuade.'[4] At twenty-four he was the deputy TGWU convenor for the East Works at Longbridge and the leading TGWU shop steward on the Confederation of Shipbuilding and Engineering Unions for the East Works.

Wright was energetic, articulate, self-assured and ambitious and involvement in the union opened up a path for him. 'You're officer material' said Harry Urwin and in 1966 he was appointed district officer for West Bromwich and the Black Country, an area with its foundries, brickyards, coalmines and backyard employers completely different from the Birmingham car industry. Much of his work was involved with personal injury and health and safety cases and he rapidly expanded the union's membership among women and immigrant workers. Just three years later in 1969 he became responsible for the chemical, engineering and motor industry in the West Midlands. In this front-line position he frequently appeared on regional television, became recognized as a rising star in the union and in 1970 he was the TUC co-ordinator in the West Midlands for the opposition to the Industrial Relations Bill, organizing and leading massive 'Kill the Bill' demonstrations in Midland cities. He had been a trade union officer for only six years when Urwin suggested that he apply for the job in Wales. It was a meteoric rise.

He came to Wales with no Welsh baggage, free of allegiances to north or south or any other factions. He came to do a job, eager to make his mark. But he did bring an outlook shaped by the industrial culture of the West Midlands, by the Birmingham car industry in particular, and by the trade unionism that had been developed there. The West Midlands was a dynamic private enterprise economy based on indigenous engineering and metal-working skills. Unlike Wales it did not depend heavily on state initiatives and public sector employment. The conjuncture of mass production by assembly-line methods, piecework systems of remuneration and fluctuations of employment in the vehicle industry had produced a trade unionism with no trace of that feeling sometimes found in Wales that employers were doing workers a favour by 'bringing jobs' to them. Trade unionism in the TGWU's region 5 was based upon the confident assertion of shopfloor power, an aggressive recruitment policy and a firm belief that Jack was as good as his master. It was these traits that Wright brought to Wales and which, allied to his personal capabilities, made him a distinctive figure in Welsh trade unionism. There were some fellow trade union leaders in Wales who regarded him with suspicion, but they recognized the reality that he would be around for a long time.

FIRST MOVES

From the moment in early October 1972 that he was asked to take on the task of setting up a Wales TUC, George Wright devoted himself whole-heartedly to the task. If he was to succeed he had to do two things: gather as much support as possible on as wide a front as possible and defy the TUC, then at the height of its power. With hindsight his strategy seems straightforward and obvious. But no one had done it before. First, he investigated the previous attempts that had failed. This was not through historical curiosity: he had been given a task that could make or break him. 'I found out why they failed, because I could not fail.' He came to the conclusion that they had failed

> because they went to London. If we want something done in Wales the instinct is to buy a ticket to London and ask their permission. In Birmingham we don't ask, we do it. If you ask London for money you won't get it if they don't like what you are doing.

This was not entirely accurate, as previous attempts had foundered in Wales before reaching London, but Wright's judgement went to the heart of the power relationships involved. If progress were to be made, a head of steam would have to be generated in Wales that London could not ignore.

His second move was to bring together people he knew would support him. Some he met in the course of his daily work. Others made themselves known as supporters of the cause. Les Paul of the Inland Revenue Staff Association (IRSF) wrote to offer his support and Glyn Phillips, a lay member of the executive of the National and Local Government Officers' Association (NALGO) was another supporter. So was Peter Jones of the constructional engineering section of the engineers (AEU). Two key full-time trade union officials who joined forces with him early on were Tal Lloyd, south Wales divisional officer for the AEU, and John Jones, district officer for the shopworkers' union (USDAW). The AEU was the second largest union in Wales and Tal Lloyd a shrewd long-serving official with a keen awareness of Welsh industrial issues besides being the dominant figure on the Merthyr Tydfil Labour council. John Jones, like Lloyd a strongly committed Labour man, was a close friend of Dai Francis, and shared with him a love of the Welsh language and frustration at the ineffectiveness of the south Wales RAC. Jones remembers Wright on his arrival in Wales as 'a young aspiring trade unionist seeking the common good. When George came he crystallized our aspirations for Wales. His aims were our aims and Dai and I decided to give him every support and backing.'[5] In a number of informal discussions Wright and the others discussed their ideas for a Welsh TUC. They wanted a body that would speak for Wales and that would have access to the highest reaches of government. They wanted a body that was truly representative of the different sectors of the trade union movement and the economy, unlike the existing RACs. It was clear also that they wanted a campaigning organization, and Dai Francis was concerned that it should co-ordinate trade union action in the eventuality of future industrial action by the miners. Tom Jones had already undertaken preliminary investigation of the advantages of such an organization in visits to Scotland and Ireland where he had obtained the constitutions and reports of the Irish and Scottish bodies. Wright also visited the Scottish TUC to discuss their constitution.

The first formal move came on 10 November when the regional committee of the TGWU, its senior district officers in Wales, and the two Welsh representatives on the TGWU's general executive council, met the executive councils of the south and north Wales areas of the NUM and Peter Jones of the Constructional Engineering Union. The aim of the meeting was 'to form a Democratic Trades Union Congress for Wales, similar to the Scottish TUC and the Irish TUC'.[6] Out of this meeting came the crucial decisions to set up a working party that would develop a suitable constitution for the new organization; and to call an all-Wales conference in Llandrindod Wells early in the new year to launch the new body. It was at this point that Tom Jones, as secretary of the north Wales RAC, received a letter dated 13 November from Vic Feather, general secretary of the TUC:

> I have noted from press reports that certain unions in Wales are proposing the establishment of a Welsh TUC, and that you are one of the sponsors. I wonder if you would be good enough to let me have details of the proposals, as we have not so far heard from any official source and it is never easy to get a complete picture from the press.[7]

Tom passed the letter to George Wright who replied on 20 November, coolly informing Feather that a decision had been taken to call a conference to examine the setting up of an all-Wales TUC, and that a working party would determine its structure, aims and objectives. He continued:

> We do not intend in any way to interfere with the existing structure of the TUC and will remain affiliated. We seek only to create a Body which will give greater expression to dealing with the problems of Wales and we would hope long term to absorb the functions of the North and South TUC RACs.

The letter closed with an invitation for a representative of the TUC to attend the first meeting of the working party on 18 December, 'if possible to give us assistance with regard to its structure in order that we may not be at cross purposes at any time'.[8] These were the first exchanges in what was to be a hard-fought battle. Wright sent a copy of this response to Jack Jones.

A basic tenet of trade unionism is that 'unity is strength'. Breakaway organizations that threaten that unity are seen as dangerous. This was one problem that the sponsors of a Wales TUC had to overcome, but with that went the issue of TUC authority. Feather saw that it was being threatened. He responded by writing separately but in similar terms, to Jack Jones and to Lawrence Daly, general secretary of the NUM, enclosing a copy of George Wright's letter and asking for their comments. He also pointed out that the general council of the TUC through its organization committee was 'about to embark on a review of the TUC's regional structure'.[9] In response to this Jack Jones, at the December meeting of his union's general executive council, gained support for the principle of establishing a Wales TUC and informed Feather of their decision. He added:

> Although recognising such a body should not supersede the general functions of the British TUC the Executive held the view that this would provide a more democratic arrangement than the existing Regional Advisory Committee set up and give a better opportunity for a more effective examination of views on, for example, Welsh economic matters.[10]

This unequivocal statement was followed two days later by a typically blunt letter from Tom Jones that set out in detail the case for the proposed 'Welsh TUC'. After pointing out the existence of the Welsh Office and its widening powers, and the decision of the Labour Party in Wales to advocate a democratically elected council for the whole of Wales, he continued:

> You will appreciate therefore, that the trade unions in Wales cannot stand still and the rank and file must be brought intos the business of running the whole of the Trade Union movement in Wales. They are aware of course, that Scotland and Ireland have their own facilities. They cannot see why trade unions in Wales should not have similar privileges to decide their own tomorrow.

Again, he emphasized the inability of the RACs, in his experience as secretary of the north Wales RAC, to represent the views of Welsh workers – 'the full-time officers had no power to make decisions' – adding that, in view of the changed situation, their function had come to an end and 'we need a better and more effective democratic machine . . . to deal with Welsh economic problems and to have one voice for the whole of Wales'.[11]

While these letters were being exchanged George Wright was busy organizing and preparing for the first meeting of the working party to be held on 18 December at the TGWU offices, 42 Charles Street, Cardiff. The composition of the working party reflected two things. First, there was the need to bring together committed supporters. It could not be said to have been a representative body. Of the fifteen present, six were from the TGWU and three were from the NUM. Peter Jones, Les Paul and John Jones were also there. Secondly, it displayed the serious intent of the TGWU and the NUM. In addition to George Wright, those from the TGWU included John Williams, the regional finance officer, and the two Welsh members of the union's general executive committee. The NUM (south Wales area) was represented by Dai Francis, Emlyn Williams, the vice-president, and George Rees (who later succeeded Francis as general secretary). George Rees was elected chairman of the working party and George Wright secretary. The south Wales RAC had met on 15 December and been informed by Wright of his intentions. These were 'noted'. It was invited to send a representative to the first meeting of the working party but did not do so. Nor did Vic Feather.

The report of the working party's meeting was subsequently circulated to all trades councils and union offices in Wales. It reflected the substantial amount of work that had been done beforehand and the seriousness with which the working party approached the project. The key decisions were that:

- George Wright would draw up a proposed constitution and standing orders for the organization (based in part on that of the Scottish TUC), which would include an annual congress and an elected general council drawn from representatives of trades councils and trades council federations as well as individual trade unions.
- This proposed constitution would be considered and debated at 'the special Congress of the Wales TUC' in February.
- All unions in Wales, all trades councils, the four federations of trades councils and the Welsh Council of the Labour Party would be invited to send delegates to that Congress.
- Trade union delegates would be invited on the ratio of one per 2,000 members in Wales; trades councils and trades council federations

could send two delegates each, and the Welsh Council of Labour would send a number to be agreed.

- The secretary, treasurer and president of the new organization would be elected by the annual congress but, after the first year, the president, who would be the chairman of the general council, would be determined by seniority on rotation so that 'even the smallest Union [could] fill a leading position within the Wales TUC'.
- The problem of financing the organization would be overcome initially by the TGWU providing office accommodation, secretarial services and equipment for the first year. The south Wales area of the NUM would sponsor, that is, pay the costs of, the initial congress. It was recognized that from time to time there would have to be a 'financial call' upon affiliated organizations to make a contribution to meet special conferences, or other circumstances such as campaigns, and to enable the trades councils to participate.
- The purpose of the Llandrindod Congress would be to elect the first officers, agree the constitution, aims and objectives of the Wales TUC, and consider the election of the general council, and the basis of that election.

These were bold, uncompromising decisions reflected in the appropriation of the term 'Congress', the confident assertion that the Wales TUC was well on the way to being a reality, and the determination to be financially independent of the British TUC. For the first year the TGWU would provide accommodation, secretarial services and equipment. Immediately after the end of year holiday, on 5 January 1973, George Wright sent out invitations to all unions in Wales to send delegates to the inaugural congress, 'a significant turning point in the history of Trade Unionism in Wales'.

On the morning of 24 January the monthly meeting in London of the general council of the TUC had before it, amongst other matters, the proposal to establish a 'Welsh Trades Union Congress'. A serious debate ensued which ended in defeat for the TGWU and the NUM. As Jack Jones wrote to Wright: 'Both Harry Urwin and I made the position of our Union clear at the meeting of the General Council and gave strong reasons why a Welsh TUC should be formed, but a number of Union leaders are very strongly opposed to the idea.' Immediately after the meeting Vic Feather wrote to the general secretaries of all affiliated unions and to the secretaries of trades councils and federations of trades councils in Wales. He informed them that the general council was undertaking a comprehensive and detailed review of TUC regional machinery and that it had already obtained the views of affiliated unions and RACs on the subject. No firm proposals had been drawn up but a discussion document had been prepared and this would be put shortly to a conference of the chairmen and secretaries of the RACs and trades council federations. The general council recognized that there may be good reasons for establishing an all-Wales trade union body and that there might be a case for making changes in Wales even if the rest of the TUC regional structure remained unchanged. There was, however, 'no case for a unilateral move in this direction before affiliated unions, through Congress, have had an opportunity of examining this matter with the care it merits'. Consequently, the general council hoped that the proposed inaugural meeting would not be held and had decided to ask the sponsors of the proposed organization, 'through the head offices of the unions concerned, to defer any further action until the general council have proceeded further with their examination of TUC regional machinery'. Finally, the general council wished to assure trade unionists in Wales that they would give 'the fullest consideration to views from representative union bodies in Wales, as well as from affiliated unions', before deciding what proposals to put to the Congress in September.[12]

THE TUC REVIEW

The fact was that the TUC had been outflanked. At its 1969 Congress Tom Jackson, leader of the post office workers' union, had successfully proposed that there should be a complete examination of the structure and machinery of the TUC.[13] This was in the aftermath of the successful, from the unions' point of view, defeat of the government White Paper *In Place of Strife*. It was Jackson's argument that the unity of purpose shown on that occasion needed to be backed by new structures that would enhance the TUC's effectiveness. Although Jackson did not refer to the TUC's regional machinery, the 1970 Congress was informed that as part of this review the general council intended to consult with RACs in order to clarify their composition, functions and needs.[14] As a member of the general council Jack Jones was obviously aware of the TUC review, and so was George Wright. But according to Wright, neither he nor Jones believed that much would come from this examination of the regional machinery. The evidence seems to support them. Two years after the Jackson resolution the 1971 Congress was informed that so much time and energy had been spent on opposing the Industrial Relations Bill in the previous year that very little progress had been made.[15] This was unquestionably a valid excuse. After another year had passed, it was reported in September 1972 that meetings had been held with RACs and 'improved contacts' would 'help to ensure that regional issues are effectively tackled'. It is absolutely clear that at this stage the inclination of Congress House was to make minor concessions to any pressures for change, and that fundamental restructuring of the TUC's regional machinery was not envisaged.[16] When, therefore, Feather wrote to Jack Jones and Lawrence Daly on 27 November 1972 pointing out that the general council was 'about to embark on a review of the TUC's regional structure', events in Wales had moved far beyond that point. The January meeting of the general council had been Feather's opportunity to place before it the Wales TUC issue and ensure that the full weight of the council was swung against the 'unilateralists'.

THE LLANDRINDOD WELLS CONGRESS

In the aftermath of the general council meeting of 24 January Jack Jones wrote to Wright and, whilst still supporting him, urged caution:

> but recognising that you and your colleagues are committed to go ahead with the conference, we think it would be advisable to secure a recommendation from the conference that the TUC be asked to consider favourably the formation of a Welsh TUC as quickly as possible and that meantime any steps to set up an organisation in final form be deferred . . . if that advice is taken we should be winning the argument in the next few months.

Wright's response to these letters from Feather and Jones was to call another meeting of the working party on 30 January. The TUC, he said, had been 'guilty of gross discourtesy' in the way it was seeking to prevent the inaugural congress from taking place. After a full discussion of the issues it was resolved that the inaugural congress on 10 February should go ahead; that the draft constitution should be discussed there and accepted 'in principle'; and significantly that another congress would be held in May. But no further action would be taken until that May congress. In the mean time, further consultations would be held with the TUC. The next day Wright wrote to inform Jack Jones of the working party's decisions and added:

I have made careful note of the points in your letter with regard to deferring a final decision. However, due to the effective work done by us in this regard, considerable support has been created and we find ourselves in a position where we are unable to defer a decision in the way you suggest . . .

It was not often that an officer of the TGWU went against the advice of his general secretary, whether that was Bevin, Deakin, Cousins or Jones. It is an indication of Wright's self-confidence that he backed his own judgement of the situation. It would be dangerous to 'go to London' and ask for favourable consideration until he had secured the backing of the inaugural 'congress' and thereby held a stronger hand. Through the momentum he had himself engendered he could argue that deferment was not possible. It was an advantage he was not going to throw away nor, in line with this tactic, did he divulge to the working party the advice he had received from Jones.

There was one further exchange with Feather before the Llandrindod Wells meeting. On behalf of the working party Wright informed him, 'We were most disturbed to find that the decision of the General Council to request us to defer the Congress had been taken on the basis of there being no consultation between us.' He then pointed out that a representative of the TUC had been invited to attend the first meeting of the working party on 18 December, and that both north and south Wales RACs had been informed of the discussions taking place and invited to participate. It was not possible to defer the congress and the working party believed that the TUC 'should send along representatives to the Wales Congress' and should enter into discussions. He added: 'I know you will be in Wales on the 10th February. Perhaps you would like to attend the Wales Congress personally – we would be happy to make the arrangements.'[17] Feather responded by asserting that the main reason the TUC had asked for deferment of further action was because the TUC was reviewing its regional machinery and 'there is no case for any unilateral move until affiliated unions, through Congress, have had an opportunity of examining the matter with the care it deserves'. Nor did he accept that there had been consultation. Although a representative of the TUC had been invited to the first meeting of the working party,

the object of meeting was, of course, to give effect to decisions already taken. I have noted that you intend to go ahead with your Congress. As the General Council have requested that it be deferred it would certainly not be appropriate for me to attend.[18]

These were the last formal communications between Feather and Wright.

Throughout January preparations for the 10 February had been proceeding. Keith Jones, who had come down to Cardiff from the TGWU's Caernarfon office to set up shop steward training in the region, was brought into the preparation team to work with Wright. In response to the TUC's advice, a number of unions declined to send official delegates, notably the General and Municipal Workers, the railwaymen and the train drivers, the steelworkers and the building workers. Against that, however, was the presence of the TGWU, the NUM, the engineers (AEU), the shopworkers (USDAW), the fast-growing white-collar union ASTMS and the major teachers' union the NUT. Altogether, thirty-five unions were represented by over 250 delegates and observers (albeit some were unofficial), as were forty-nine of the fifty-three trades councils in Wales and the four trades council federations. The Welsh Council of Labour was represented by its secretary J. Emrys Jones, and by D. J. Davies and Jack Brooks. Wright had invited all the Welsh Labour MPs but none turned up. The most enthusiastic was John Morris (Aberavon) who was prevented by family illness from attending. He nonetheless wrote: 'I know how effective the Scots are as trade unionists in being able to demand audience from the Prime Minister down. I saw it as a Minister. We need in Wales, working as part of the TUC, a national body for Wales.'[19]

The congress was held in that venue for so many other all-Wales meetings, the Metropole Hotel, and in a move by Wright designed to ensure support from the AEU it was chaired by Tal Lloyd.[20] In opening the meeting Lloyd declared that there was 'no desire or intention to break totally from the British TUC'. The thrust of Wright's opening speech was that the time had come for a democratic body 'representative of the whole of the movement in Wales' to defend Wales against the social and economic neglect of recent years. In the subsequent debate fifteen speakers took part, all except one of whom were in favour of a Wales TUC. When the vote was taken on acceptance of the working party's report 'in principle' only three people voted against. George Wright was elected secretary.

It is not clear however what the delegates were voting for. Some were undoubtedly voting for a totally independent TUC for Wales, whilst others wanted a more democratic and more effective voice for trade unionists than the existing RACs. The working party report could be interpreted either way and its ambiguity left Wright with a largely free hand. He could stress the determination and unity of those who were for a new organization, yet argue that Welsh trade unionists desired unity with the wider movement. Armed with the Llandrindod decision he anticipated entering into negotiations with Victor Feather over the relationship between a Wales TUC and the British TUC. Accordingly, on 20 February, he wrote to Feather informing him of the Congress's decision and added: 'We wish for genuine consultation to take place as soon as possible for we are required to report back to a further Conference in May of this year.' Feather saw it differently. In no circumstances would he negotiate with an unofficial body that was acting in defiance of the general council. Henceforth, all his communications were with organizations registered with the TUC.

THE TUC INITIATIVES

On 24 March he unveiled to the chairmen and secretaries of the RACs and trades council federations in Britain detailed proposals for reforming the TUC's regional structure, including membership for lay members and representatives of trades councils as well as full-time officers. The number of TUC regions in England would be reduced from twelve to eight to coincide with the government's economic planning regions. The possibility was also raised of appointing full-time TUC officials in the regions to back up the new bodies. Most delegates from England welcomed these ideas as being a long overdue revision of the machinery. The Welsh delegates saw, however, that the proposals fell far short of those already agreed at Llandrindod Wells in which the Wales TUC would have an annual conference, an elected general council or executive and a much greater involvement of trades council representatives.

On 13 April Feather convened a conference of unions with members in Wales. Each union was invited to send up to three representatives to the conference[21] and on behalf of the TGWU Jack Jones nominated Tom Jones, George Wright and himself. The conference provoked considerable debate among the 116 delegates who attended. A document prepared by the TUC's organization department noted that the establishment of a Welsh Office and a Secretary of State meant that the case for establishing an all-Wales trade union body, instead of two RACs, was considerably strengthened. It went on to say that there appeared to be no reason why the new regional machinery envisaged by the TUC should not also be adopted in Wales. In introducing this document the TUC general secretary acknowledged Welsh national sentiment but argued that any new organization should be part of the TUC. Anything else would lead to fragmentation rather than unity. In the debate that followed, arguments for

a Wales TUC were strongly put by a number of delegates who also emphasized that the Wales TUC and the British TUC would work closely together.
Jack Jones was among those who forcibly made the case along these lines.

Those who spoke against the idea of a Wales TUC, of whom the
leading figure was Sid Greene of the NUR, argued that it had been taken
forward in an undemocratic manner with only a few unions invited to
sit on the working party and most being faced with a *fait accompli*. The
machinery suggested by the TUC for the regions would be fully capable
of representing the needs of trade unionists in Wales. Most tellingly, it
was pointed out that the proposals for a Welsh TUC were vague about
how the body would be financed in the long run. A new Wales trade union
body outside the British TUC would have to raise finance separately. Yet
some unions were already in financial difficulty and would be unable to
afford subscriptions to a trade union organization other than the TUC.
The meeting ended with Len Murray, the assistant general secretary,
acknowledging that the existing RAC structure in Wales was outmoded
and that there was a strong case for one body for Wales. The TUC would
want to hold further discussions before making any final decisions to be
put to its congress in September, but its proposals for new regional
machinery offered the maximum degree of unity.

George Wright now faced a dilemma. The TUC showed no interest in
consulting with him or the working party about developments in Wales
and the second 'congress' called for 12 May was fast approaching. He
needed to be able to report progress and take on board the 13 April discussion, particularly the financial issue. This was discussed at a meeting
of the working party on 18 April where the necessity of funding by the TUC
seems to have been accepted, with the details to be negotiated by Wright. He
next invited the north and south Wales RACs to meet him on 4 May to
review the situation. The TUC had accepted that there should be one
regional body for Wales, so this was agreed with the added provision
that the trades council federations would receive representation, a point
not in the TUC scheme. They agreed that the new organization would be
named either the Welsh Council of the TUC or the Wales Trade Union
Council. More controversially, future consultations on the new structure
would be held between the TUC and the two RACs and the trades council federations. George Wright, of course, was a member of the south
Wales RAC. Graham Saunders wrote to Len Murray on 7 May saying, 'I
believe substantial progress was made at this meeting, and it was clearly understood that any future discussions would be held within the
machinery of the TUC.'

The second congress of 1973 met at the Royal Pier Pavilion, Aberystwyth, on 12 May. There was some tidying up of the proposed constitution, principally the deletion of all references to the Wales Council of Labour in order to meet the objections of those unions, like NALGO, that were not affiliated to the Labour Party. But the main issues were the decisions agreed at the meeting with the two RACs. The fundamental question of the financing of the Wales TUC by the TUC rather than by affiliation fees from the unions with members in Wales was accepted with little debate. Again it was left to Wright to discuss the details with the TUC. But Congress unanimously rejected the notion that the working party would not be involved in future negotiations with the TUC. The lengthiest debate came on the proposed name for the new organization. Eventually the proposal by Glyn Williams of the NUM that it should be 'Welsh Congress of Trade Unions' was agreed. Wright, who by now was clear that the TUC as the funding body would not authorize the use of the term 'Congress', argued for 'Wales Trade Union Council'. After all, it could be abbreviated to Wales TUC.

Matters were now coming to a head. Two 'congresses' representing a strong body of opinion in Wales had affirmed a determination to set up an organization for trade unions radically different from the prevailing arrangements. The TUC's latest proposals were moving in the Welsh direction. Most Welsh Labour MPs were in favour, with Cledwyn Hughes and John Morris providing strong support, as were the Plaid Cymru MPs. George Wright was busily briefing newspaper correspondents and the campaign had a high head of steam. Victor Feather, as TUC protocol required, would not communicate with the leaders of the proposed Welsh Congress of Trade Unions. Yet, with summer holidays looming and arrangements for the September Congress in Blackpool being finalized, he needed to ensure that the proposals for reform of the TUC's regional machinery, including that in Wales, would be accepted. The Blackpool Congress would be his last before retiring and there was a natural desire that everything should go smoothly. A point had been reached where agreement was preferable to deadlock.

To make progress he called a meeting at Congress House on 12 June for the chairmen and secretaries of the RACs and federations in Wales to meet the TUC's organization committee. Up to that point TUC officials – principally Feather himself and Len Murray the assistant general secretary – had conducted discussions with Welsh representatives. But the organization committee was composed of fourteen members of the general council, a number of them general secretaries of their own union.

Several of the committee were already persuaded of the case for a Wales TUC: Alf Allen of USDAW who had been convinced by John Jones (and who that year was chairman of the general council); Edward Britton of the NUT; Cyril Plant of the IRSF; Audrey Prime of NALGO; and Harry Urwin and Fred Howell of the TGWU. The committee was left in no doubt about the strength of feeling in Wales. The meeting began with the representatives from Wales expressing disappointment that the working party had not been invited. 'This, they argued at some length, would not be conducive to the success of the discussions, as they understood that the object of the meeting was to attempt to reach some accommodation between the respective proposals put forward by the TUC and the working party.' Once that point had been countered with the comment that 'there could be no doubt about the competence of the representatives [present] to express the views of trade unionists in Wales', the discussion shifted to the substantive matters in dispute. The discussion was both lengthy and at times heated. Some delegates continued to make the case for a Wales TUC similar to those in Scotland and Ireland. Others agreed that the TUC proposal to replace the two RACs with one body for Wales had merit and that it should be possible to reconcile the two positions by careful discussion. But neither point of view accepted the TUC proposal as it stood. The strength of opposition, and the fact it was backed by conference decisions at Llandrindod Wells and Aberystwyth, persuaded a majority of the organization committee that there would have to be a change in the official TUC line. The meeting ended therefore with an understanding that the organization committee and the general council would give further consideration to how the TUC's proposals for regional reorganization could be adapted to Wales. Moreover, 'it might be necessary for further consultations to take place'. On one point the committee did not give way. They were adamant that the term 'congress' could not be used, as this would only lead to 'confusion'.[22]

Unquestionably the exposure of the members of the organization committee to fiercely expressed grass-roots opinion made this a key meeting. Events now moved swiftly. As a parting shot the Welsh representatives had suggested that Cardiff would be a good venue for any 'further consultations' and they would be happy to convene such a meeting. A meeting was therefore arranged for 3 July in Cardiff. Significantly, Vic Feather now dropped out of the discussions and the TUC officials were Len Murray and Ken Graham, head of the organization department. Even more significantly, the TUC agreed that the federations and RACs could appoint additional representatives. This enabled members of the working party to be present at the meeting in Cardiff.

But before the meeting there was work to be done. D. Ivor Davies, secretary of the Glamorgan Federation of Trades Councils had campaigned for many years for a Wales TUC and in the 12 June discussions had forcibly argued the case. In addition to keeping Wright abreast of what had transpired, he now urged all trades councils to inform the TUC that they rejected the TUC proposals and fully supported the decisions taken at Llandrindod Wells and Aberystwyth. On 29 June he wrote to Wright expressing his concern that the TUC's proposals for the forthcoming meeting were 'identical with their proposals and attitude at the London meeting on June 12th'. The TUC, he noted, was still opposed to the use of the word 'congress', was against the idea of an annual conference with directly elected delegates, wished to approve the appointment of a chairman and in fact was still holding to its conception of regional machinery as proposed for England.[23]

Despite these concerns, substantial progress was made at the 3 July meeting. Wright and Murray had by then informally discussed the situation on several occasions, concentrating on the areas of most agreement. Although a tough negotiator, Murray, with his Shropshire roots, had a better feel than Feather for Welsh affairs. In a private meeting in Congress House Murray and Wright reached agreement on most of the issues. The Cardiff meeting reflected this spirit of compromise and agreement. The TUC representatives recognized that any machinery established by the TUC in Wales would need to have the confidence of trade unionists in Wales and should not be imposed. On the other hand, the Wales TUC proponents accepted that it was neither practicable nor desirable for a section of the trade union movement to seek to establish and operate a separate organization without the support of the TUC or affiliated unions. With these principles agreed, the way was cleared for progress on a number of points. There would be one trade union body for Wales and that would be called the Wales Trade Union Council. The finance for that body would be provided by the TUC. There would be an annual conference instead of quarterly meetings as proposed by the TUC. A general council, chairman, secretary and treasurer would be elected by that annual conference. The education services provided by the TUC would continue to be separately provided by the TUC (as they were in Scotland).

Two areas were left outstanding. One was the proportion of trades council delegates to union delegates at the annual conference. The

TUC wanted it to be 25 per cent, the Wales TUC constitution agreed at Aberystwyth had offered 40 per cent. In discussion the Wales TUC representatives suggested 33 per cent. The other issue was the composition of the general council. In order to involve a wider range of unions the TUC wanted a much larger body than the thirty envisaged in the Wales TUC constitution. A majority of the Welsh delegates suggested an enlargement from thirty to forty-five, with thirty coming from the unions and fifteen from the trades council side. On 5 July George Wright, in a letter to Len Murray, emphasized that the suggestions from Wales were 'accepted by an overwhelming majority of the trade unionists in Wales'. On the same day he wrote to Jack Jones and Harry Urwin informing them of the situation and hoping that they would be able to get support on the general council for the Welsh point of view.[24] They did. At the July meetings of the TUC's organization committee and the general council the Welsh proposals were accepted.[25]

What, then, was the end result of all these negotiations? The Wales TUC that emerged was not a Welsh Trades Union Congress separate from the British TUC but a regional council of the TUC. This outcome was inevitable once it had been accepted that its finances would have to come from the TUC. But its constitution was significantly different from those of the English regional councils. It had an annual conference, which they did not. It had a greater representation of the grass roots – the trades councils – on its governing bodies than they. The delegates to the annual conference were elected; the delegates to the English quarterly meetings were nominated. The word 'congress' did not appear in the formal title but neither did the word 'regional'. 'The Wales TUC' rapidly became common usage. It had the right to take its own decisions on Welsh matters and the constitution democratically agreed at the Llandrindod Wells and Aberystwyth 'Congresses' remained substantially intact.

Given the devolutionary activity in Wales in the early 1970s, the pressures from the NUM and the pugnacity of D. Ivor Davies and other trades council representatives, would a Wales TUC have emerged anyway without the intervention of the TGWU? The answer must be: not at that time and not in that form. A challenge to the TUC required resources that the trades councils did not have. The NUM nationally and in south Wales was embattled, with closures and a falling membership. The key steps in the founding of the Wales TUC were the merger of two TGWU Welsh regions into one in 1968, the growing appreciation by Tom Jones that the economic problems of Wales required a much stronger trade union voice, the appointment of him as the first all-Wales TGWU regional secretary, and the subsequent appointment of George Wright to run the Welsh region and bring a Wales TUC into being. Behind each move was the vision and authority of Jack Jones. This was a deployment of resources beyond the reach of the grass roots and unmatched by any other union in Wales. And there was no other trade unionist in Wales with the energy, boldness and confidence of Wright. His urgent advocacy of the case for Welsh trade unionists to be involved in economic decision-making seemed to some to indicate that he 'had gone native'; that he had been infected with Welsh nationalism. They missed the point. It was a Birmingham trade unionist speaking: employers should not be allowed to get away with anything. 'You were equal to the employers; they were not better than you. I believed that when anyone took a decision about Wales the unions should be there, not to be consulted, but because we had things to offer, a job to do.'[26] In the confrontation with the TUC, the combination of Jack Jones and George Wright pushed it as far as it could go at that time. Despite the gloss put on events by the TUC's official account, there were those in Wales (and on the TUC general council) who were convinced that without the Wales TUC initiative the TUC would not have gone as far as it did in revising its regional machinery in England.[27]

THE END OF THE BEGINNING

The inaugural meeting on 27 and 28 April 1974 at Aberystwyth was held in a celebratory mood. The 259 delegates[28] were not just celebrating the launch of the Wales TUC. The miners had recently won another national strike – 'a piece of cake' compared with 1972 said Dai Francis, reflecting the new spirit of unity among Welsh trade unionists – and in the process the Heath government had been brought down. Harold Wilson was back in Downing Street, Welsh MPs were prominent in the Cabinet, and the trade unions and the government were working together to produce a 'social contract'. Len Murray, now TUC general secretary, conducted the conference until the election of Dai Francis as chairman. Francis's good humour and determination that all should go smoothly earned him the nickname 'Dai Unanimous'. George Wright was elected part-time secretary. Two topics dominated the debates: devolution and the Welsh economy, the delegates clearly understanding the significance of one for the other. The Kilbrandon Report on the constitution was welcomed with a call for the setting up of an elected legislative assembly for Wales, able to deal 'with the many industrial, economic and social problems confronting the Principality of Wales, but without a reduction in the total number of Members of Parliament'. The main subject of debate, however, reflected in a variety of motions, was the gathering storm about the economy. The size of the task ahead of this new body was plain when the conference issued a clear call for the steel-making plants in Wales to be kept open. It was to be the centrepiece of the Wales TUC's campaigning for the next six years.

Chapter 3

A Campaigning Organization

We do not sit like sitting ducks waiting for disaster to come. (Leo Abse)

The delegates celebrating at the inaugural conference in April 1974 could not have known that trade union power was nearing its post-war zenith, or that the revitalized alliance between the unions and the Labour government would end in the recriminations of the Winter of Discontent. The minority Labour government that came to office in February 1974, with a miners' strike still in progress, soon settled it on terms that gave substantial increases. In the October election Labour secured a small but clear majority. The Trade Union and Labour Relations Acts of 1974 and 1976 repealed the Industrial Relations Act and restored traditional trade union legal immunities. The Health and Safety at Work Act 1974, the Social Security Pensions Act 1975, the Sex Discrimination Act 1975, and the Race Discrimination Act 1976 provided workers with new rights and protections. The Employment Protection Act 1975 placed the Advisory, Conciliation and Arbitration Services (ACAS) on a statutory footing.

But the economic scene was less satisfactory. Prices were rising rapidly, primarily due to the oil crisis of 1973, and so were earnings. There was a sense that matters were moving out of control. By August 1975 the annual rate of inflation was 26.9 per cent. For some months it had been evident that the agreement between the unions and the government – the Social Contract – was not capable in its existing form of restraining inflation. Inevitably, in the midst of the crisis, a pay policy was cobbled together and increases were limited to £6 a week for adult employees during 1975–6.[1] A second phase of the policy, agreed by the TUC despite its aversion to cuts in public expenditure, limited wage increases to 5 per cent all round with a lower limit of £2.50, and an upper limit of £4.00.[2] But a run on sterling in the autumn of 1976 led the government to borrow from the International Monetary Fund and adopt policies requiring further public expenditure cuts. In September 1977 the

TUC called for an immediate return to free collective bargaining. The government, however, announced a target of a 10 per cent limit on earnings and promised to use sanctions against employers who exceeded the limit. For 1978–9 the government, again acting without TUC support, announced a 5 per cent pay limit at a time when inflation was running at over 8 per cent. That winter the norm was breached by a series of strikes involving Ford workers, oil tanker drivers, and road haulage drivers. A wide range of local government and public sector manual workers then went on strike, including ambulance workers, dustmen, water and sewerage workers, and gravediggers. The impact on public opinion was considerable. On St David's Day the devolution referenda in Wales and Scotland failed to deliver. On 28 March 1979 the government lost a vote of confidence. In May the Conservative Party, led by Mrs Thatcher and pledged to attack trade union power, achieved electoral victory.

The events from 1974–9 set out above were the central concerns of domestic industrial relations and politics throughout those years. They affected all workers and were the backdrop to the early years of the Wales TUC. But important as they were, these were not the chief concerns of that new organization. The British TUC was dealing with the government on those matters: even so, the Wales TUC gave it every support. At a Cardiff meeting with Callaghan in 1978 leaders of the WTUC pleaded with him to add just 1 per cent more to the pay norm in order to 'sell it' to the members. Callaghan steadfastly refused, pleading 'Treasury advice'. But the central task of the Wales TUC was to be the voice of Welsh workers on issues that arose in Wales, and the most pressing of these was the loss of jobs in coal and steel.

THE PARLIAMENT OF LABOUR

But how credible was this new organization? It had no full-time staff of its own and depended heavily upon the TGWU for resources. Its 'office' comprised two rooms in the TGWU's Cardiff office in Charles Street. Its shorthand typist for twenty hours a week, Eleri Shaw, was employed by the TGWU, as was Keith Jones the administrator. Above all, its public face and general secretary was the irrepressible regional secretary of the TGWU. Without this help the Wales TUC could not have been up and running as a working organization. But it was not surprising that to some the Wales TUC looked like a wholly owned subsidiary of the TGWU.[3]

There was considerable substance to that view but it was not the whole story. The constitution of the organization, unlike the previous RAC arrangement, opened up involvement to a broad range of unions and lay members. Like that of the British TUC it provided for an annual conference and elections to a general council – where bloc votes would count and where horse-trading of support could take place – a democratic scenario familiar to the officers of large unions. The smaller unions too had a place in this arena and those with more enterprising officers – such as ASTMS – were able to work the system and acquire a higher profile than their numbers may have justified. The presence of trades council delegates at the general council and conference ensured a lively input to policy formation. Personalities also played a part in the initial stages, for with strong characters like Dai Francis as chairman and Tal Lloyd vice-chairman, and through them the involvement of the NUM and the AEU, it is hard to maintain that the interests of the TGWU always predominated. Moreover, the scale of work envisaged involved all forty-five members of the general council in committee work.

But most important of all for its legitimacy and authority, government ministers including those at Cabinet level opened their doors to it. In the first nine months members of the general council met, on separate formal occasions, the Secretary of State for Industry, the Secretary of State for Wales, Lord Crowther Hunt (to discuss devolution), and Lord Beswick twice (to discuss the steel industry). And early in its life a Cabinet Minister offered a resource that would raise its profile higher still.

On 5 August 1974 Anthony Wedgwood Benn (as he was then known), the Secretary of State for Industry, wrote to Wright saying that he had been asked to approve a research grant to Professor Ken George at University College, Cardiff. 'I have suggested a different way of handling this project', Benn wrote:

> instead of funding this project I should offer the money to you in the Welsh TUC – about £20,000 – and ask you whether you would consider how that money might be spent in a way that would be most helpful to us and your members . . . I would be happy to discuss the matter with you since I attach great importance to this and hope that you will feel able to respond positively. Once we have agreed a programme the money will be made available.[4]

Wright responded immediately, informing Benn, 'you may rest assured you will receive a positive response from the Wales TUC'. Despite applications from Professor George at Cardiff, and a team from the Polytechnic of

Wales, the Wales TUC chose the Trade Union Research Unit (TURU) at Ruskin College, Oxford, to run the project. TURU had proven industrial relations and economic expertise and a record of working for the trade union movement. In addition, in Dennis Gregory they had a staff member who had worked with Wright in the Midlands on shop steward and full-time officer training and who, under his auspices, had written a paper on the Welsh economy for the Llandrindod Wells congress. The broad aims of the research were to be

> to provide the Secretary of State and the WTUC with a detailed analysis of the economic problems of the Welsh Region and the underlying theme will be the relationship between the changing economic conditions in Wales, the flows and structural shifts of industry, and the socio economic needs of the people of Wales. Particular emphasis will be placed on the disproportionate importance of steel in Wales that is to say the fact that steel accounts for the biggest single proportion of manufacturing employment.[5]

Out of the blue the WTUC had acquired a resource that enabled it to capture the headlines as report after report came from the research team, Denis Gregory and John Atkinson. Between March 1975 and December 1977 they produced a total of twenty-three papers (see Appendix 1) as well as a number for internal discussion only. Strictly, it was not academic research. Most of the papers were based upon published government statistics and the authors did not hesitate to be polemical. On the contrary, 'We tried to be challenging and campaigning.'[6] But their carefully argued submissions required answers, contributed to Welsh Office thinking and in some cases spurred government action. They provided bullets for Wright to fire and, as Keith Jones remembers, 'We were setting the agenda because we were coming up with stuff that no one else had.' Suddenly there was a new player on the Welsh political scene, representing and expressing the interests and aspirations of nearly half a million Welsh workers and their communities.

Benn's diary reveals that his initiative went against the advice of his permanent secretary, contributed to a major departmental row and upset the TUC.[7] His direct approach and offer of funds to the Wales TUC (constitutionally a TUC regional council) gave it a degree of autonomy that the TUC found unwelcome. Moreover, it was not TUC policy to accept money from government, any government. Only in this way, it had traditionally argued, could it maintain its independence. Before the details of the research project had been finalized, Len Murray, much to the annoyance of members of the Wales TUC general council, asked that no action should be taken until the Department of Industry had 'fully disclosed its plans for the grant' to the TUC.[8] According to Wright, Murray was against the Wales TUC taking the money. When told, 'We don't have to ask you. We're taking it anyway,' David Lea, the head of the TUC economic department, who was present, exclaimed 'We've lost our virginity!' Within a year the TUC lobbied government for public funds to support trade union education and received a grant of £400,000 for the year 1976–7.[9]

But it was John Morris, the Secretary of State for Wales, who emphasized the authority of the WTUC by calling its annual conference 'the parliament of organised labour in Wales' and in the same speech referred to his relationship with it as being one of partnership:

> Since I took office as your Secretary of State my door has been an open door. I have been on two occasions to meet your General Council. Your officers have been to my office from time to time and perhaps the importance of the very act of the creation of this great new body has been underlined by the very fact that your officers were able to talk to the Secretary of State day in and day out and, what is more important I am able to speak to your leaders in the same way . . . We will discuss, we will argue; we will agree and we will differ, but at least it will be a great partnership because we will all be working for Wales.[10]

No pressure group could ask for a more explicit acknowledgement of its legitimacy and authority. This 'external' acknowledgement, visible from its earliest days, enhanced the 'internal' authority exerted by the WTUC in relation to its constituent unions, who were happy to be involved in an organization that provided them with a new platform and access to the Welsh Office, government ministers and various public bodies.[11]

The range of issues discussed by the WTUC was, from the beginning, extremely wide. At its second meeting the general council discussed: the steel industry, devolution, the location of Hirwaun gas tanks, Rhoose airport, toll charges in Wales, vehicles for handicapped persons, Cefn Seidon Bay, the Employment and Training Act, Celtic oil and trade union organization within Wales. Discussion for discussion's sake was not, however, the style of this organization. The energy that had been released by its formation looked for achievement and in the early years, through conference resolutions, research papers, special conferences and meetings with ministers and civil servants, it campaigned on a variety of issues. Some of the more significant were: devolution, the development of Rhoose airport, the health service, housing in Wales, the EEC, the need for the Graig Goch reservoir, racism, compensation for industrial lung diseases and local government finance. On Rhoose airport, the Graig Goch reservoir and industrial lung diseases it campaigned successfully. It failed to carry the day in its opposition to EEC membership in the referendum of 1975 and also failed in its support for a Welsh Assembly in 1979. Other issues, such as the health service, housing and local government finance, remain contemporary and contentious. But the campaign that absorbed most time and energy was the state of the Welsh economy, particularly the rundown of the coal and steel industries.

THE CRISIS IN STEEL

The crisis in the British steel industry during the 1970s had a profound impact upon the Welsh economy and labour force. Unemployment in Wales was 3.6 per cent in 1974, by 1984 it was 15.6, and job losses in the steel industry accounted for over one-third of the total unemployment growth in that period. Taking the knock-on effects into account that proportion rises to over 50 per cent.[12] For example, the cutbacks in steel caused a decline in the demand for coking coal. Twelve pits were closed and 8,000 miners left the south Wales industry in the period 1972–9. By 1984 a further eight pits had closed and another 7,000 wage earners had left. Taking into account the substantial pit closures of the 1960s, a fundamental change had taken place in the structure of Welsh industry and in the character of its labour force. Hardest hit was the heartland of the Welsh labour movement: the heavily unionized, comparatively well paid male manual workers of south Wales.

Inevitably the trade unions resisted the closure of steelworks and the loss of jobs but the Wales TUC had no more success than the individual unions in the steel industry or the TUC itself. They all failed. From a trade union point of view it was a fight that had to be fought; but in the process much was revealed about the relations between the WTUC and the TUC, and about the fundamental weakness of the trade union 'movement'. The restructuring of the industry began in 1966 when, in response to low profitability, the Benson committee as part of a general review recommended that steel making in Wales should continue at Port Talbot, Llanwern and Shotton, but that there should be phased closures at Brymbo, Ebbw Vale, East Moors, Briton Ferry, Llanelli and Gowerton. When in 1967 substantial parts of the steel industry were renationalized only the small Briton Ferry and Llanelli steelworks in Wales were left in private hands. The Heath government's White Paper of 1973 envisaged the closure of all publicly owned steel-making sites in Wales, including Shotton, leaving only Port Talbot and Llanwern, where there would be modest investment and some expansion of output. This attempt to make the industry competitive through eliminating the older plants is now seen as both optimistic and misguided. The whole European steel industry suffered from gross over-capacity through an inability to compete with new works in Japan, south-east Asia and Latin America. When Britain entered the European Economic Community in 1972 finished steel from Europe entered the home market, a situation exacerbated by a declining home demand for steel and British Steel's decision to 'sacrifice quality for quantity'. Imports of finished steel rose from 6 per cent of the market in 1970–1 to 20 per cent by 1978–9 and the BSC continued to incur massive financial deficits: £255m in 1975–6, £93m in 1976–7, £444m in 1977–8, £309m in 1978–9 and £545m in 1979–80. The problems went back to the way the industry was nationalized and were compounded by mismanagement.[13]

The impending closures in steel therefore dominated the early years of the WTUC. The first meeting of its economic and industrial development committee reviewed the 1973 White Paper and emphasized that priority should be given to social considerations against narrow commercial ones. Throughout 1974 the campaign gathered momentum. Meetings were held in Cardiff and London with Lord Beswick who, on behalf of the Labour government, was reviewing the White Paper. The Research Unit produced a paper on the social consequences of steel closures that received wide media attention and broadened the union agenda to include the potentially damaging effects steel closures would have on already hard-pressed communities. Discussions were held with the action committees at the threatened works, and the issue was raised with the Secretary of State for Wales. Some success was achieved when in 1975 Lord Beswick postponed by four years the closure dates for East Moors and Shotton but accepted that iron and steel making (not tinplate production) would be wound down at Ebbw Vale over 1975–7. The review did not put the problems to rest. The workers at Ebbw Vale were bitter about their situation; the Steel Corporation, increasingly in debt, wanted more and faster manpower cuts; in Port Talbot, where 2,300 jobs had been lost through cost cutting, there were fears that the proposed expansion would not take place; and at Shotton there was deep concern that the plant was to be closed to enable Port Talbot to expand. The Wales TUC strove to maintain harmony between the two groups, emphasizing that the problems of the industry were a national and not a north v. south issue.[14]

The cuts in public expenditure meanwhile began to cause unemployment and the WTUC did not hold back in its criticism of the government. A research paper in September 1975 argued that cuts in local government expenditure would result in lower standards, fewer services and lower manning levels. As local authorities in Wales had far more pressing and serious problems than many authorities in the rest of the UK, the cuts were inequitable. In October 1975 the executive went to Downing Street and expressed the Wales TUC's concern about rising unemployment to Harold Wilson, the Prime Minister, and other senior ministers. British Steel continued to push aggressively for further substantial cuts in manpower. By January 1976 more than 5,500 steelworkers in south Wales were on unofficial strike as managers unilaterally cancelled shifts. An agreement between the Corporation and the unions on 22 January recognized the urgent need for voluntary redundancies but postponed the threat of compulsory redundancies for at least three months.[15] In conceding the urgent need for manpower reductions and placing negotiations on manning levels at the plants concerned, the agreement abandoned any national policy of resistance and opened up a way for closures to be accelerated.

By April 1976 the Wales TUC Conference was calling upon the government to halt all steel closures until suitable alternative employment was available in the areas affected, and deploring the inadequate action taken by the government to combat escalating unemployment. Although there was some feeling that the WTUC should be organizing demonstrations, the general view in the spring was that lobbying and presenting arguments to ministers were more effective than demonstrations.[16] Slowly the mood changed. At the August general council meeting the view was expressed that unemployment levels in Wales were completely unacceptable and that the government was in danger of taking for granted the loyalty of the trade union movement. Unemployment and public expenditure cuts were placed top of the agenda in the forthcoming meeting with the Prime Minister. It was also agreed to hold conferences where Wales TUC policies concerning unemployment could be put to members and affiliated organizations. Its submission to Callaghan as Prime Minister in October 1976 declared:

> We reject explicitly government policies which will savagely erode job opportunities in what has hitherto been a vital growth area for employment . . . The government should be warned that we are implacably opposed to any

reductions in the standard or frequency of services offered by the public sector and that our full backing will be given to recognised trade union action against the proposed cutbacks.[17]

In the autumn a new problem arose with the expected closure of Courtaulds factories at Flint and Dowlais. Despite representations to ministers, both plants closed in 1977. In February 1977 Len Murray joined with George Wright in speaking at WTUC meetings organized in Flint and Cardiff, and throughout 1977–8 there was continued pressure on ministers, meetings with the rank-and-file action committees, and conferences in north and south Wales with ministerial and trade union speakers. Again there was some success. Investment in continuous casting at Port Talbot was given the go-ahead. Closures at Shotton were deferred and Deeside was given Development Area Status. At the end of 1977 the research unit produced a document, *Unemployment: The Way Out. A Ten-Year Strategy*, that argued that economic growth would provide no more than a partial remedy to the problem of unemployment. In addition to growth the paper argued for a reduction in the labour supply through six measures: early retirements, sabbatical leave entitlement for all workers, work experience/training for 16–19 year olds, control of overtime, paid educational leave and a basic thirty-five-hour week.[18] Without such measures there would continue to be a surplus of labour over requirements. This document too received wide media attention at the time.

Nonetheless, the steel closures continued. Iron and steel making in Michael Foot's constituency at Ebbw Vale finally ceased in 1978. In the rundown over 5,000 jobs were lost. The end came too for East Moors, Cardiff, in Jim Callaghan's constituency, where almost 4,000 lost their jobs. These closures, together with a combination of early retirements, non-recruitment, productivity deals and the closure of the private Briton Ferry works, resulted in almost 20,000 lost jobs during the 1970s.

Throughout this period the WTUC continued to have access to Cabinet Ministers, met the Prime Minister annually, and was able to present the case against steel closures and for its alternative economic policies. It argued for participative planning machinery in Wales, a strong regional dimension to industrial policy, selective import controls, the deferment of steel closures until new jobs could be found, more and better industrial training, the movement of civil service jobs out of London and into Wales, and measures to bring the supply of labour in line with demand. Despite these ideas being in line with TUC thinking and the 1974 Labour Party Election Manifesto, there was little chance of them being adopted. The Treasury's main concern was belt-tightening, even before 1976.[19] Industry policy was watered down considerably after Benn was shifted to the Department of Energy in June 1975, and the crisis in steel seemed unstoppable as BSC's deficits mounted. But the arrival of Mrs Thatcher in May 1979 brought a much colder climate altogether.

THE CRISIS DEEPENS

The Thatcher government was committed to a drastic reduction of the public sector borrowing requirement and an emasculation of trade union power. The steel industry as a massive borrower of public money was one of its first targets. It was also one of the industries singled out by Nicholas Ridley as a potentially successful battleground for the Tories against the unions.[20] Sir Keith Joseph, the Industry Secretary, announced in June 1979 that the industry would have to break even in 1980–1. It was an impossible target that was later relaxed but it forced the BSC into another massive round of cutbacks. In November the seven-year fight to retain steel making at Shotton ended and 6,400 jobs were lost when the plant closed in 1980. On 11 December the BSC announced that steel capacity would be cut from 21.5 million tonnes to 15 million tonnes; exports would cease; and there would be a total reduction of 53,000 in the labour force within eight months. Wales would bear a major part of the cuts. In addition to the Shotton closure, up to 15,000 redundancies were sought from Port Talbot and Llanwern, either by closure of one of them or a sharing of the burden between them. In turn there would be major implications for the tinplate works at Trostre and Velindre.

The reaction in Wales was one of outrage. On the day the cutbacks were announced George Wright saw Len Murray to discuss ways in which trade union opposition to the closure plans could be rallied. The next day he warned that if the government did not intervene a general strike was 'a possibility' and sent a telegram to Mrs Thatcher urging her and senior ministers to visit south Wales. She refused the invitation. Philip Weekes, the NCB area director, warned that halving steel production at Port Talbot and Llanwern would also halve BSC's consumption of south Wales coking coal, and affect more than 8,000 jobs. Dafydd Elis Thomas, MP for Meirionydd, wrote to George Wright urging

a dramatic initiative that will force the Government to turn back on its deter- mination to subject the working class in Wales to the merciless forces of the market system . . . I am well aware that political opposition at the parliamentary level alone cannot force any changes and it may well be time to consider industrial action beyond the steel unions themselves. A day of action to defend jobs in Wales, organised by the Wales TUC, would I am certain attract massive support.[21]

Six days later the leaders of the coal and steel unions in Wales agreed on an all-out strike in Wales unless the BSC's plans were suspended for two years. They also demanded the suspension of Sir Charles Villiers, BSC's chairman, and his three senior executive officers, and the appointment of a caretaker management pending a special inquiry into the Corporation and its commercial activities. The Wales TUC general council gave full backing to these demands and declared that if they were rejected then an all-out strike of all unions involved would begin on 21 January 1980.[22] Meanwhile an emergency meeting of the executive of the south Wales area NUM decided to press the national executive to call a nation-wide strike against pit closures. The miners had already gained the support of the Newport dockers who were refusing to unload two ships carrying 18,000 tonnes of United States coking coal destined for Llanwern. To complicate the picture even more, ten days earlier, on 7 December 1979, the executive of the largest union in the steel industry, the Iron and Steel Trades Confederation (ISTC) had voted to begin national strike action on 2 January 1980 over its pay claim. At a time when inflation was running at over 17 per cent, the union had been offered a 2 per cent increase.

The ISTC duly went on strike on 2 January. The National Union of Blastfurnacemen came out on the same day and the TGWU joined in on 4 January, followed by the craft unions on 9 January. All BSC steel and tinplate works in the UK were shut down and the WTUC was threatening an all-out strike of steel, coal and transport workers commencing on 21 January. An urgent round of meetings followed, involving the TUC steel committee, the TUC nationalized industries committee, and the Wales TUC. On 10 January the TUC nationalized industries committee considered the Wales TUC's urgent request that the BSC's closure plans and its plans for imported coal should be included in the steel strike demands. On the advice of the TUC's steel committee the request was turned down and the WTUC was urged to delay the 21 January strike to allow time for extra talks with the BSC and the government. In the face of this heavyweight opinion (the nationalized industries committee included general secretaries of the most powerful unions) the WTUC agreed to postpone the all-out strike until 'on or about' 10 March, but determined to go ahead with a one-day general strike on 28 January. It also reaffirmed its support for a total blockade against coking coal entering through the south Wales ports. Even this was a step too far for a majority on the TUC general council. In a statement it sympathized with the situation in Wales and expressed deep concern about the prospects for south Wales if 'the twin issues of steel closures and coal imports were not resolved soon'. It emphasized, however, that 'it was essential that leadership and authority should be exercised by the General Council' and that any future action should be decided on a national (UK) basis.[23]

There was now a clear rift between the trade union leaders in London and those in Wales. The ISTC had called the national steel strike over the issue of pay and that alone. In the eyes of the TUC, the programme of closures announced by the BSC, affecting plants in England and Scotland as well as Wales, was a separate issue. It was to be pursued by the TUC along the well-worn path of making representations to the government and to the BSC in order to achieve 'a more realistic timetable' for the closures. In Wales perceptions were different. Years had been spent in discussions with ministers, arguing without success against the closure of pits and steelworks. Thousands of jobs had been lost, and now the future of the only two remaining modern steelworks was threatened, and with them a large part of the coal industry. Wales TUC researchers estimated that BSC's plans would lead to the possible closure of twenty-one pits and a total loss of 50,000 jobs. The time had come to make a stand and the steel strike offered that opportunity. It was feared that if the pay issue was settled before the job cuts were successfully resisted, the steelworkers would return to work and not come out again to defend jobs. This was the reasoning behind tying the two issues together. In George Wright's view, the steel strike in Wales was 'about jobs and pay – in that order'. Emlyn Williams, area president of the NUM, declared 'Survival is more important than wages' and went on record to say, 'My loyalty is with the Wales TUC. We are fighting to prevent the Welsh nation from being de-industrialised.' Commentators freely spoke of levels of unemployment comparable to the 1930s with accompanying social deprivation, emigration of the young and the break-up of communities.[24] A confidential BSC internal memorandum conceded: 'The scale and rapidity of the necessary manpower reductions in south Wales is of a magnitude *never* encountered before in a relatively small geographical area.'[25] The result, as the Committee on Welsh Affairs duly reported, was a 'jobs chasm into which the economic and social structure of large parts of Wales are in danger of falling'.[26]

Tom Jones, secretary of the first all-Wales region of the TGWU who, with the backing of Jack Jones, unilaterally declared that there would be a Welsh TUC. (Photo: Keith Jones)

George Wright, newly arrived in Wales, surveys delegates' support at the unofficial inaugural congress at Llandrindod Wells, February 1973. (Photo: George Wright)

Dai Francis (NUM), who joined in that unilateral declaration with Tom Jones, addressing the 1975 conference from the chair. To his left is Tal Lloyd.
(Photo: Wales TUC)

Tony Benn, who as Secretary of State for Industry provoked a departmental row by giving the Wales TUC £20,000 for research into Welsh economic problems.
(Photo: George Wright)

John Morris, Secretary of State for Wales, tells the 1975 conference: 'You are the Parliament of organized labour in Wales.' (Photo: Wales TUC)

John Jones (Usdaw) addresses the 1976 conference in Welsh. To his left is D. Ivor Davies. Both were early supporters of the Wales TUC.
(Photo: Wales TUC)

Len Murray, general secretary of the TUC 1973–1984, after initial reservations came to admire the achievements of the Wales TUC. (Photo: George Wright)

Sylvia Jones, first woman to chair the Wales TUC, who led the delegation that met the new Prime Minister, Mrs Thatcher, in 1979.
(Photo: Wales TUC)

Michael Foot, leader of the Labour Party and MP for Ebbw Vale, addressing the 1981 Porthcawl conference on the catastrophic return of mass unemployment.
(Photo: George Wright)

Emlyn Williams, president of the south Wales area of the NUM during the 1984–1985 miners' strike, forcibly makes his point, as always.
(Photo: George Wright)

James Callaghan, Prime Minister and MP for Cardiff South, appeals for
wage restraint at the 1977 Tenby conference.
(Photo: Wales TUC)

David Jenkins, general secretary of the Wales TUC 1983–2004, who had to contend
with 'the Dark Age for trade unionism' from 1979 to 1997.
(Photo: Wales TUC)

Peter Hain, Secretary of State for Wales and MP for Neath, continues the tradition for Labour Cabinet ministers to address the Wales TUC conference. (Photo: Wales TUC)

Felicity Williams, general secretary of the Wales TUC from May 2004. (Photo: *Western Mail*)

Yet the scale of the problem was not fully appreciated in London. The TGWU in Wales had a substantial membership in steel and tinplate, but for the union as a whole the numbers were not significant. A major part of the South Wales Coalfield was threatened with closure but the national executive of the NUM did not accept that as a reason for a national strike. The TUC steel committee did not see the need to tie the issues of pay and jobs together, quite apart from the doubtful legitimacy of doing so. Moreover, the Wales TUC's call for all-out strike action not only cut across the TUC's belief in the value of operating in the corridors of power, but also raised the issue of whether the WTUC had the authority to do so. In Wales the TUC stance was seen as weak and remote. There was a strong feeling that, with the retirement of Jack Jones and Hugh Scanlon, there was a leadership vacuum on the general council. In fact, Len Murray was sympathetic to the stance taken by the Wales TUC, believing the jobs problem to be the main issue. But the TUC had no power to interfere in the bargaining role of the ISTC and it had to maintain constitutional proprieties. The WTUC on the other hand prided itself on being closer to the people and on reflecting the views of a nation that had never given the Tories a parliamentary majority. It was time for Wales to stand against the Tories, and for the Wales TUC to be in the vanguard.

The one-day strike (also known as 'a day of action') went ahead on 28 January with the Wales TUC claiming that 110,000 people came out on strike and that upwards of a quarter of a million workers throughout Wales took part in demonstrations. Its focal point was the march through the centre of Cardiff of 15,000 trade unionists with banners flying, headed by the Markham Colliery Band. Amongst the banners one encapsulated the issues: 'For Sale: one South Wales coalfield. Agents: the British Steel Corporation.' A packed rally in Sophia Gardens pavilion was addressed by Michael Foot, George Wright, Lawrence Daly, the general secretary of the NUM, and Bill Sirs, general secretary of the ISTC, who was so affected by the occasion that 'I could not prevent tears of emotion rolling down my cheeks.'[27] In a statement the WTUC declared:

> The wanton destruction of our major industries cannot be allowed to proceed unchecked. The feelings expressed in Wales on January 28th should be seen as but a first step along the road to securing economic and social policies suited not to the 1930s but to the 1980s.

Three days later a 'high level' TUC delegation met Geoffrey Howe, Chancellor of the Exchequer, Keith Joseph, Secretary of State for

Industry, and other ministers. Other meetings followed, but essentially the government refused to intervene in the strike or in the closure programme and the TUC was diverted into discussions with the EEC and BSC that continued long after the strike had ended.[28] The Wales TUC general council, meeting a week after the successful one-day strike, had to consider its next move. To take further action on a Wales basis alone would have limitations, yet there was widespread disquiet that the campaign would effectively be lost once it was taken over by the TUC and the national executives of unions. In a lengthy and heated debate Emlyn Williams and George Rees for the NUM argued forcibly that, rather than hand matters over to the TUC, the Wales TUC should capitalize on the success of 28 January and plan for a more prolonged stoppage. In the end the meeting tried to face both ways by voting to accept the TUC's approach, but also kept open the possibility of taking local action. To ensure full consultation with the membership it also decided to have a special conference on 27 February at which the TUC general secretary would be invited to speak.[29] In effect the indefinite strike pencilled in for 10 March had been called off. The TUC through its various committees would continue negotiations with government ministers and EEC officials. One result of these negotiations was that on 11 February the BSC and the National Coal Board reached an agreement that the BSC would not import any additional coal in 1980. Ann Clwyd, a member of the European Parliament, then arranged for a combined TUC/WTUC delegation to lobby the European Parliament's Social Affairs and Employment Committee and the EEC Commissioners D'Avignon and Vredeling. This was organized for 21 February to be followed by a meeting with Sir Keith Joseph on 25 February.

The miners' leaders now took matters into their own hands. Thousands of jobs were at risk yet their national executive and the TUC had declared that strike action on 10 March would be unconstitutional. It was not a stance that accorded with the south Wales miners' tradition of left-wing leadership and militant action. Emlyn Williams was forthright, 'when it comes to catastrophic effects on unemployment to hell with the constitution. I believe that the people in the leadership are too constitutionalised.' Nor was he impressed by the agreement between the BSC and the NCB on coal imports, for pit closures and redundancies were still threatened by the plans to halve steel production in Wales. Self-interest as well as trade union solidarity determined that the steelworkers could not be left to fight alone. A delegate conference voted unanimously on 20 February to join the steelworkers in an all-out strike from 25

February. It was confidently expected that the delegates' decision would be endorsed at pithead ballots over the next two days, a mere formality. It was not. The strike call was overwhelmingly rejected. Newport dockers in response lifted their blacking of a ship carrying American coking coal. The rejection stunned the area leadership. They had been complacent about the pithead ballots; the NCB had not been. Philip Weekes, the south Wales director, was in the midst of efforts to find other markets for coking coal 'to ensure we save pits and jobs. I earnestly urge South Wales miners not to damage these objectives, but to give us all a fighting chance.' In the prevailing atmosphere of insecurity, it was his voice that was heard.[30] It was a turning point. The shock troops of the Welsh working class had refused to go into battle.

On the day set for the miners' strike that did not happen, 25 February, a delegation from the Wales TUC met Keith Joseph and Nicholas Edwards, the Secretary of State for Wales. It was not a satisfactory meeting. As George Wright reported to the general council three days later, Keith Joseph was not well briefed and appeared vague. Nothing helpful had come out of it. The mood of the general council was one of disquiet. Not only had it, under pressure from the TUC, called off the proposed strike on 10 March but also the recall conference scheduled for 27 February. Yet there was little sign that the TUC was making progress on the closure issue. The TUC opposition to a recalled conference was also resented as an attempt to frustrate democracy and to deny the representatives of unions in Wales the opportunity to debate the crisis publicly, its causes and consequences. Nonetheless, it was agreed once more not to recall the conference. Instead, it was decided to seek a meeting with Len Murray and the executives of unions in order to discuss a positive programme of action.

There was no such meeting. But on 17 March Len Murray attended a special meeting of the general council where the frustrations boiled over on both sides. (Significantly no representatives of the NUM or of the ISTC attended.) Murray began by explaining that the TUC had rejected a recalled Wales TUC conference because the media could present such a conference as a split within the trade union ranks, and unity was essential. With thousands of jobs lost and thousands more at risk it was an argument that cut little ice. Members reminded Murray of Bevan's famous reference to 'the unity of the graveyard', while others referred to the Wales TUC's loss of credibility as a result of having to chop and change policies and decisions in recent weeks. Many more spoke of increasing demoralization within south Wales as the campaign to save jobs was seen to be floundering. On several occasions Murray was asked what contingency plans the TUC had made in case talks with BSC failed. His response was to point out the constitutional position of the TUC, and incidentally of the Wales TUC itself. This was that, even if the TUC wanted to, it was not in a position to call strike action. That was a matter for individual union national executives and what had become apparent during recent months was that the Wales TUC had failed to get its message across to affiliated unions and their executives. The Wales TUC had asked, indeed demanded, that the TUC take the lead in this issue. Just because it was not entirely satisfactory, it was wrong to talk of circumventing that lead. It was time for the Wales TUC to fall in line.

The tensions within the trade union movement that had built up over the preceding months were reflected, and to some extent deflected, at the Wales TUC conference at Llandudno in the first week in May. The south Wales area NUM submitted a motion that deplored

> The fact that unions affiliated to the Wales TUC hide behind National Union Constitutions to enable them not to implement the decisions taken by the Wales TUC General Council . . . the Wales TUC was originally created to protect and deal with the economy of Wales, and to co-ordinate any action necessary to ensure that the job opportunities in Wales do not suffer as a result of government policies.

If debated this would have brought into the open the tensions between the TUC and the Wales TUC, and also between the NUM south Wales area and some other unions in Wales. In the event the motion was withdrawn following much backstage pressure and an impassioned speech by George Wright in which he told the miners that the Wales TUC was 'Still demanding from the TUC that they should work with us to settle the problems which face you and the problems which face the steelworkers and the problems that face all the related industries and those in other industries as well.'

In the same speech his frustration with the attitude of the TUC and the constraints placed upon the Wales TUC was made crystal clear:

> When we face a crisis of a 50,000 job loss in one year, inflicted upon us by wicked and incompetent managements, supported by a callous and vindictive government, I don't believe that we have to trudge to London to ask anybody what we have to do about it, it comes from within us what we have to do . . .

we expect a greater measure of self-determination and we would like you [the TUC general council] to give some thought to that, particularly when we face problems such as we face.[31]

By then the steel strike, the longest official strike since the 1930s, had ended on 3 April. A Committee of Inquiry recommended an 11 per cent increase across the board, plus 4 per cent from local productivity deals, plus other measures that made a total of 15.95 per cent. In the course of the dispute Granada television alleged that the government had pressurized the BSC to make its original low offer, presumably in the belief that the steel unions would not have the stomach for a fight at a time when redundancies were taking place. When the strike ended the TUC was still pressing the BSC to agree to short-time working and other labour-saving measures. Within days, local negotiations on slimming down the workforces at Port Talbot and Llanwern began. By mid-May workers at Port Talbot had agreed on job cuts and a redundancy package and a similar agreement came at Llanwern in late June. The 'slimline' solution meant that 6,883 jobs disappeared at Port Talbot and 4,545 at Llanwern. That was not quite the end of the matter.

Soon after Ian MacGregor became chairman of the British Steel Corporation in May 1980 the threat of total closure of either Port Talbot or, probably, Llanwern, was revived, with fears of dire effects on Welsh coking coal production. This sparked another round of hectic activity. All through the summer the Wales TUC attempted to develop 'a programme of persuasion' but found that neither MacGregor nor the Welsh Group of Conservative MPs were willing to meet its representatives. The miners – their leaders having learned the lesson of the debacle in February – agreed through pithead ballots a policy of total opposition to pit closures, except where coal reserves were exhausted. At the end of July the cross-party House of Commons Committee on Welsh Affairs published a scathing report in which it deplored the continued emasculation of steel capacity in Wales. It quoted with approval a statement by the secretary of the Wales TUC that there were very real possibilities of disorder unless matters were handled with sense and gentleness. The government largely ignored the report.

Also in July Murray and Wright met and agreed that Wales should play a leading part in the national campaign against Tory government policies. In August a meeting of the steel and coal advisory committee of the Wales TUC discussed the severe demoralization in the steel industry and the threat of further pit closures. It was agreed, amongst other measures, to seek a meeting of the TUC nationalized industries committee in Cardiff 'to ensure that the TUC was fully appraised [sic] of the situation in Wales'. In October at a conference of 140 delegates from steel, coal, rail and engineering unions, Wright admitted that there were seemingly insurmountable difficulties in generating an industrial response to closures. The only two alternatives left were 'acceptance or community based resistance'. Four days later, at a general council meeting, he again spoke of the possible need for a more broadly based community response including, if necessary, an element of civil disobedience.[32] The closure of Port Talbot or Llanwern would have catastrophic effects on the Welsh economy and had to be resisted at all costs. The call was met with a lukewarm response. What did it mean? There was vague talk of blocking the Severn Bridge by a slow-moving convoy; or of some action akin to the refusal of Plaid Cymru members to renew their television licences which, with Gwynfor Evans's hunger strike, had forced the government into a U-turn over the issue of a Welsh-language television channel. But did the Wales TUC have the ability to organize such a campaign? The credibility of the organization would be at stake if threats were made and not then delivered.

The proposed meeting with the TUC nationalized industries committee came on 17 November when it met the Wales TUC's general council and its steel and coal advisory committee in Cardiff. A morning's discussion ensued on the state of the Welsh economy and the following resolution was adopted: 'This meeting warns that any attempt by the British Steel Corporation to close either Port Talbot or Llanwern would result in industrial action which would have the support of the Wales Trade Union Council and the TUC.' In the afternoon the TUC committee and members of the Wales TUC general council were joined by representatives of the nationalized industries in Wales, the Wales CBI, the Council of the Principality, and Labour MPs including the Opposition Spokesman on Wales. Again, a full discussion took place on unemployment and the dangers posed to the Welsh economy and the need for the government to implement the report of the Committee on Welsh Affairs.[33]

This put to bed talk of civil disobedience, vague as it had been. At its December meeting the Wales TUC general council 'accepted that the campaign surrounding both the threat of civil disobedience and the prospect of trade union inspired community based resistance had served its purpose'. The threat of such disorder had always been recognized as a tactic as opposed to a realistic outcome and it was equally recognized that there was a real danger that such advocacy could become counter-productive.

It was therefore agreed 'that it would be tactically sound to play down this issue in the coming period'.

In the end both major steelworks remained open. The privately owned Duport works at Llanelli closed in 1981. By 1983 the BSC had only 19,199 employees in Wales, compared with 65,981 in 1973. Altogether, in ten years almost 50,000 steel jobs had disappeared. The earlier predictions of the WTUC's researchers, criticized in some quarters as alarmist, had proved to be stunningly accurate.

THE LESSONS OF FAILURE

The most common explanation for the failure to halt closures is that steelworkers 'took the money and ran'. In other words the fundamental problem was the large sums of money that the BSC was offering to workers as redundancy compensation. These sums, up to £20,000 in some cases, undermined the workers' will to resist closure. As Bill Sirs explained:[34]

> How *can* you get workers, many of them in their fifties, some of them in debt, others needing a new car or new furniture or a holiday, to turn down huge sums of money and instead fight the employers with tough, sustained industrial and political action? The fact is, you cannot.

Unquestionably, as closure followed closure, this is what happened. But it took place in the context of years of uncertainty about the future of jobs, continuing BSC financial deficits, lack of investment and local negotiations for closure in which the TUC steel committee, once brought into a plant by the workforce, saw its role as driving the hardest bargain possible for the workforce.[35]

The conventional trade union response to the threat of closures throughout the 1970s was to lobby for delay until alternative work was available in the affected areas. This was never going to materialize in the numbers and skills required but some delays were achieved. The Wales TUC and the British TUC through its steel committee and its national-ized industries committee were at one in this process. When a closure seemed inevitable, then compensation for redundancy became the subject of plant bargaining. Whilst participating enthusiastically in the lobbying process, it is clear through its research papers that the Wales TUC was keenly aware of problems inherent in the process. These were plant chauvinism encouraged by BSC statements and illustrated graphically by the rivalry and bitterness between Port Talbot and Shotton; the inadequacy of the alternative employments that were provided; and the short-sighted acceptance of money for jobs.[36] But the major rift came with the closures announced by the BSC in December 1979.

The outcry from the trade union grass roots, as well as from politicians of all parties, provided the Wales TUC with a platform for radical action. It responded by pressurizing the TUC to make the closures part of the steel strike, by organizing its one-day strike and by threatening an indefinite strike from 10 March unless its demands were met. The TUC, by contrast, continued to depend on traditional lobbying methods and rejected the Wales TUC's plans for further militant action while promising to throw its weight against the closures. Given that only the national executives of trade unions could have sanctioned official strike action, it is evident that the Wales TUC was attempting to punch above its weight. Yet it was firmly believed in Wales that, at the least, concessions could be wrung from a government obviously rattled by the Welsh reaction.

There is reason to believe that the Wales TUC was right in this judgement. There were three critical moments. The first came in November 1979 when, in the face of further demands for job losses, the normally amenable ISTC could take no more. Bill Sirs, its general secretary, went to the TUC steel committee and proposed an embargo on all overtime work in BSC plants; a national lobby of Parliament including a twenty-four-hour national steel stoppage; further selective strikes in the steel industry; and no further negotiations on severance and redundancy payments. The thirteen other unions on the steel committee refused to back the proposals.[37] It was this failure on the part of the steel unions to put up a united front that enfeebled the TUC response and undermined the stance taken by the Wales TUC. The second occasion came early in January 1980 when the national executive of the NUM refused to back the south Wales area call for a national strike, apparently on the grounds that only south Wales was at risk. The third occasion came a month later when the leaders of the south Wales area of the NUM broke ranks with the Wales TUC, voted for strike action alongside the steelworkers and then found that they were leaders without an army.

On all three occasions it can be argued that militant action could have won concessions from the government. This belief arises from the events of February 1981 when, in response to threats of more pit closures, half of the South Wales Coalfield came out on unofficial strike, swiftly followed by the Kent and Scottish miners. Other areas followed their lead, and an official NUM national strike was imminent. At that point the Prime Minister herself intervened and the NCB was ordered to withdraw its closure proposals. The Chief Secretary to the Treasury, John Biffen, said on television: 'The spectre that frightened the government was the very clear evidence that there would be massive industrial action.'[38] In this light the three occasions mentioned above were lost opportunities. The miners' strikes of 1972 and 1974 were still fresh in the minds of the new Conservative government and a major confrontation with an alliance of public sector unions was, at that stage, to be avoided at all costs. The Cabinet still contained a number of influential 'wets', including Jim Prior the Secretary of State for Employment.[39]

The fact remains, however, that while concessions could have been won, they would have been just that. The government surrender to the NUM in 1981 was followed by the victory of 1984–5. Steel closures may have been further delayed in 1980, but they were not halted altogether. Militant and united action in 1980 would have been at best an act of defiance against the acceleration of closures. For the previous decade the steel committee had been accepting the closure logic of the Corporation's campaign.[40] It had not fought tooth and nail against the BSC strategy because to do so would have required the steel committee to have a vision, an alternative plan for the development of the industry. This it did not have, and this was the fundamental weakness of the steel unions' position.[41] Consequently the Wales TUC, with the steel unions, was always fighting a long-run losing battle. But with more than 40 per cent of employees in Wales in the public sector, including the nationalized coal and steel industries, the Wales TUC was in the forefront of the struggle. It was this that set Wales apart from most other areas in Britain, that generated a passionate resistance in 1980, and which national union executives and the TUC did not have the imagination and courage to support.

Chapter 4

The Enemy Within?

The pendulum never swings back to the middle. (Dai Francis)

The victory of Mrs Thatcher in 1979 was not unexpected, but there were few in the trade union movement who fully grasped its significance. Many thought it would be a temporary interruption – like 1970–4 – to a settled period of Labour rule that had begun in 1964. Nor was 'Thatcherism' as an ideology the dominant force in 1979 that it soon became. Len Murray recalled:

> We thought that this was another Conservative government and we had had plenty of Conservative governments in the past and we'd got on with them, you know, reasonably well. And we saw no reason why we shouldn't get on with Mrs. Thatcher reasonably well.[1]

As late as two years after her victory the Wales TUC produced *Social Plan: A Bargain,* a 'consultative document' that proposed the abolition of private education, major reductions in working hours, the preservation of closed shop agreements, the planning of incomes and a range of measures to promote sustainable economic development. The proposals were designed to be part of an agreement between the Labour Party and the unions and clearly did not envisage the Thatcher government holding power for very long. The *Plan*, largely the brainchild of George Wright and drafted by Denis Gregory, drew fierce criticism from the National Union of Public Employees (NUPE) and the south Wales area of the NUM. Both argued that it was not sufficiently socialist in content and contained at its core a national incomes policy, the subject that had divided the trade unions and the Callaghan government. The fact that delays in the drafting meant that it did not go to the general council before being put before the conference did not help its passage. A fractious conference referred the document back to the general council. In 1982 a much amended document emerged entitled *Planning the Future – Economic Recovery and Beyond.*[2] But this document too looked forward to the election of a Labour government at the next general election.

The 1983 election result put an end to these delusions. Mrs Thatcher's attitude towards trade unions was already clear but in 1984 she put it more starkly: 'In the Falklands, we had to fight the enemy without. Here the enemy is within, and it is more difficult to fight, and more dangerous to liberty.'[3] For the rest of the 1980s and into the 1990s the trade union movement wrestled with the political and economic consequences of Thatcherism. Eighteen of the Wales TUC's first twenty-three years were spent with a Tory government at Westminster, a fact that inevitably curbed its development. Yet in an administratively devolved Wales it had opportunities for positive achievement in ways that distinguished it from the TUC.

A SINGLE-MINDED ATTACK

The Conservative attack on the trade unions unfolded on three fronts: major changes to employment law; a free rein given to market forces with an acceptance of rising unemployment; and a sustained removal of union influence in policy arenas. The legal changes came with remarkable rapidity in a series of Acts – the Employment Acts of 1980 and 1982, the Trade Union Act 1984, the Wages Act 1986, the Sex Discrimination Act 1986, the Employment Acts of 1988, 1989 and 1990. These Acts were consolidated in the Trade Union and Labour Relations (Consolidation) Act 1992 and followed by the Trade Union Reform and Employment Rights Act 1993. Their overall effect was to regulate union activities in previously unheard of detail, severely curtail the unions' bargaining power and ability to take legal strike action, remove from individual workers many areas of employment protection and shift power substantially in favour of employers.[4]

The 1980s brought the worst economic recession since the 1930s. Unemployment increased from one million in 1979 to 3.1 million at the end of 1982. It stayed at over 3 million until 1987, fell back to 1.5 million by the end of 1989, but by early 1991 it exceeded 2 million and reached almost 3 million again by early 1993. These levels were recorded despite numerous changes to the definition of unemployment in order to make it seem less than it was. The return of mass unemployment in 1979–82 was influenced by a worldwide recession but the government's fiscal policy and the effect of North Sea oil upon the exchange rate were more significant. The second major recession beginning in 1990 was largely due to government increases in interest rates and entry into the European exchange rate mechanism. The significant fact about the recessions, however, was that the government took no steps to mitigate the levels of unemployment. As Keith Joseph asserted in 1979, 'full employment is not in the gift of government. It should not be promised and cannot be provided.'[5] But unemployment was an acknowledged consequence of the government's economic policy. John Major brutally pointed out: 'If the policy isn't hurting, it isn't working.' The return of mass unemployment provided the ideal environment of fear and insecurity in which the legal measures could work effectively and managements assert their authority. Allied to these changes in the labour market was a calculated product market upheaval in the highly unionized nationalized industries and services. The privatization of telecommunications, gas, water, electricity, buses, docks, airports, railways, steel, British Airways and British Leyland reduced the number of employees in nationalized industries from almost two million in 1979 to less than half a million in 1993, with consequent exposure to competition and changes in working practices. The overall effect of these changes was to make trade unions and collective bargaining marginal to the conduct of industrial relations throughout the private sector.[6]

Just as relentless was the erosion of trade union political influence built up over a hundred years. TUC officials and senior union leaders continued to meet ministers but it was made clear to them that these were not negotiations but meetings at which ministers would explain their position.[7] Increasingly, contacts took place at a lower level and face-to-face meetings declined steadily. The practice of making trade union leaders members of government inquiries, committees and commissions ceased. From being Churchill's 'Fifth Estate', the TUC reverted to being one among many pressure groups, and a largely unsuccessful one at that. Gradually, too, TUC representation on tripartite bodies was downgraded. The National Economic Development Council lasted until 1992 but a number of training boards and the National Enterprise Board disappeared in 1980. Over the next eleven years the contribution of trade unionists to manpower policy was progressively severed. The Manpower Services Commission was wound up in 1988. Taken together this three-pronged strategy – legal, economic and political – represented 'probably the most single-minded and sustained attack on the position of a major and previously legitimate social force to have been undertaken anywhere under modern democratic conditions'.[8]

The unions and the TUC were completely unprepared for such an onslaught. At first they did not believe that Mrs Thatcher would do what she proposed – break the post-war consensual acceptance of trade unions and collective bargaining, and install a regime of economic liberalism. Their initial response was to protest, expecting that the policies would change. A TUC 'Campaign for Economic and Social Advance', in which the Wales TUC played a full part, advocated an alternative economic strategy. In 1981 and 1983 there were People's Marches for Jobs and in those early years a variety of demonstrations and days of action were organized. None of them deterred the government from its path. After Labour's largest post-war defeat in 1983, when more trade unionists than non-trade unionists voted Conservative, Len Murray argued that the unions had to come to terms with the new world and accept aspects of the legislation. Even this approach was scorned by Mrs Thatcher, whose determination to take on the miners and to ban unions at the GCHQ signals centre at Cheltenham in 1984 hastened Murray's early retirement. The defeat of the miners in 1985, followed in 1986 by the success of Rupert Murdoch in breaking the influence of the print unions confirmed the new balance of power.

THE MINERS' STRIKE

This is not the place to give an account of the year-long strike that unexpectedly began in March 1984. That has been done elsewhere, although definitive accounts remain to be written.[9] The most significant dispute of the post-war period, it was manufactured outside Wales by Margaret Thatcher and Arthur Scargill, class warriors on a collision course. Ostensibly a strike against pit closures and the rundown of the coal industry, it was a political confrontation in which the government spent over £2.5 billion to defeat a union whose president declared: 'We want to save our jobs. But more – we want to prepare the way for a transformation, rolling back the years of Thatcherism.'[10]

Unlike the earlier campaign against steel closures, the involvement of the Wales TUC was marginal, for reasons largely outside its control. At the beginning of the strike Peter Heathfield, NUM general secretary, told the TUC: 'no request is being made by the Union for the intervention or assistance of the TUC. Should such be required I shall further contact you.' It was six months before the NUM asked for formal assistance at the September TUC Congress. But at the beginning of the strike the south Wales area approached the Wales TUC for help. On 21 March the general council agreed to give full support and in June held a major march and rally in Cardiff attended by thousands. Its main involvement, however, was in relations between the NUM, the transport unions and the ISTC. From the start of the strike, the NUM national leadership aimed to halt steel production as part of its larger strategy of reducing the country's industrial output. They therefore sought help from individual unions, particularly the lorry drivers and dockers in the TGWU, the railwaymen and the seamen, in attempts to blockade the integrated steelworks. It was a move guaranteed to antagonize the ISTC, which understandably was determined to maintain what remained of the industry and its membership. However, south Wales steelworkers gave their support to the rundown of coal stocks at the steelworks, although coal continued to be docked at Port Talbot. Then a deal was struck that allowed coal to be delivered by rail from the docks at Port Talbot to the Llanwern steel plant in return for which the steelworkers cut their normal output by 25 per cent. Consequently, steelworkers lost their production bonus payments, accounting for over 40 per cent of their total earnings.[11] Nonetheless, it worked well, with the Wales TUC playing a co-ordinating role, until the national NUM leadership in June 1984 ordered a complete halt of supplies to steel plants. Kim Howells, picket organizer for the NUM south Wales area, saw the result:

> The steelworkers reacted angrily and the Triple Alliance disintegrated. The following week brought an awesome and depressing sight: massive convoys of scab haulage firms roaring between Port Talbot and Llanwern on the M4 . . . As many as two hundred lorries would frequently be lined up under heavy police escort to make the hazardous run. The M4 became ochred with the dust of iron ore and its bridges filmed with small-coal.[12]

Steel production rocketed and acrimony within and between unions increased. In the strikes of 1972 and 1974 a major reason for the success of the NUM had been the support of other unions. The divisions within the NUM created by the failure to hold a national ballot on strike action, combined with the reckless tactics of the national leadership, alienated members of other unions in 1984. The decision of the NUM to conduct the strike from its Sheffield headquarters also marginalized the role of the Wales TUC. The president of the south Wales area informed the Wales TUC on 19 June that he did not wish it to assist in the implementation of agreements and arrangements.

On 1 August 1984 all south Wales area NUM bank accounts, including its food funds, were frozen because of the union's refusal to comply with an April court order barring its secondary picketing at Port Talbot steelworks. The Forest of Dean firm Read Transport, with contracts to carry coke from Port Talbot steelworks to various destinations including Llanwern, had obtained an injunction to prevent the NUM picketing the works. The picketing had continued. The road hauliers took the issue to the High Court with the result that the south Wales area was fined £50,000 for contempt of court and its assets were sequestered. For the next seven months the south Wales area survived without access to any of its funds. The fact that it did survive speaks volumes for the communal support it received and for the fund-raising efforts from within as well as outside the formal labour movement. The TGWU, NUR and NUPE among others found ways, not always official, of supporting the miners. At the request of the NUM the Wales TUC established a Hardship Fund on 31 July 1984. When it was closed on 24 May 1985 just under £114,000 had been donated to food and relief purposes in north and south Wales. In the inevitable recriminations that followed the return to work in March 1985 there were allegations that the Wales TUC had not worked hard enough to achieve solidarity during the strike. A proposal at the south Wales NUM executive committee on 23 April that the union should withdraw from the Wales TUC was only defeated by the casting vote of Emlyn Williams.[13] The executive did decide, however, to second a motion put down by Swansea and District Trades Council for the WTUC May conference, criticizing the WTUC's 'lack of leadership' in rallying support for the miners amongst Welsh workers. In the event it did not support the motion, and chose in the debate to direct its criticisms at the British TUC. The motion was heavily defeated.

The fact was that the aims of the strike and its conduct were never clarified. For Scargill it was an all-out war against the state. When in December 1984 the TUC refused to back the NUM in its total defiance of the courts he branded British unions as class traitors. In south Wales it began with reluctance as a strike against pit closures – a majority of pits voted initially against action – consolidated in loyalty to the union and developed into a struggle for community survival. For the TUC the tactics of the NUM leadership undermined the support it could muster from its constituent unions. As Norman Willis, Len Murray's successor as general secretary of the TUC, said at the notorious meeting at the Afan Lido in Port Talbot on 13 November 1984 when a hangman's noose was lowered in front of him, 'the TUC is not an army and I am not a field marshal'. The tactics of the NUM leadership were also outside the industrial relations experience of the TUC. In that same speech Willis declared: 'anyone who genuinely cares about the future of the mining industry – and the government and the NCB have repeatedly said that they do – knows that there must be a genuine negotiation and a genuine agreement, and the sooner the better'. But despite consistent efforts by the TUC in January and February to broker an agreement, the NUM executive rejected all offers. So long as the south Wales miners were solidly behind the strike, as they remained throughout, a majority of the national executive were prepared in the words of George Rees 'to fight to the last drop of south Wales blood'.[14] The return to work, without agreement, was initiated by the leaders of the south Wales miners who were appalled at the drift and lack of leadership shown by the national leaders. The fact that the strike was sustained for a year in the face of a massive state and employer offensive reflects the community solidarity that it inspired both within and outside the coalfields. (Among the cheques that poured in was one for £2,000 'for the Welsh miners' from Sir Alec Guinness.) There was widespread respect for what the mining communities had achieved and anger at the ruthless tactics of the government. In Wales it was a further step for many towards a consolidation of Welsh identity and the frustration that arose from rule by a government that had the support of comparatively few in Wales. Devolution came back on the political agenda. A slogan painted on a railway bridge in Ron Davies's Caerphilly constituency read: 'We voted Labour – we got Thatcher'. The strike, however, saved neither the coal industry nor the miners' union.

LIVING WITH THE TORIES

Nor did it have a long-lasting effect upon relationships between the government and the Wales TUC. Each by then knew where the other was coming from. But it took time for understandings to emerge. An early experience came when a delegation from the Wales TUC met Mrs Thatcher in 1979, primarily to press the case for keeping the Shotton works open. She received them charmingly, exchanged pleasantries with Sylvia Jones – the WTUC chairperson – about the fact that they were both mothers of twins, proceeded to dominate the meeting, listened carefully to the arguments about Shotton and then ignored them. She did not meet the Wales TUC again.

In that first year, contact with the Welsh Office diminished considerably. George Wright reported to the 1980 conference: 'The only time we are ever consulted on any matter affecting the people of Wales is when we raise a question with them.'[15] Meetings were held, however, with the new Secretary of State Nicholas Edwards. The first meeting soon after the election in 1979 was a frosty and awkward affair. Edwards spent the best part of an hour avoiding eye contact by steepling his hands and staring fixedly at the ceiling as Wright and other WTUC leaders attempted to engage him. The contrast with John Morris's open door could not have been clearer. 'It was evident that there were many and deep policy differences between us with regard to future economic and social policy in Wales.'[16] The meeting over steel closures with Edwards and Keith Joseph, the Secretary of State for industry, was equally unproductive. Later in 1979 Edwards refused to meet the WTUC to discuss new technology. Throughout the period of Tory rule the Welsh Office door was never closed, though nor was it open to the same extent as under Labour and on a number of occasions various Secretaries of State refused to meet the WTUC. When they did meet there were clear limits to the influence that the WTUC could exert. After the 1983 election the strategy explicitly became one of working at the margins of government policy – the areas where the Welsh Office had discretionary powers. Even there, however, topics such as pensions, education and health were not susceptible to influence.

It was a dispiriting period. David Jenkins, who in May 1984 succeeded George Wright as general secretary, admitted in January 1985 at the height of the miners' strike: 'As the government cannot be influenced on its main lines of policy, there is a general demoralisation and a feeling of "does it matter what we say?" '[17] It was a question that echoed, in very different circumstances, George Woodcock's 'What are we here for?' In the 1960s Woodcock wanted the trade unions to recognize that the days of street protests were over and that 'the TUC should use its influence in the committee rooms sitting opposite the men with power in government'.[18] In the 1980s the men (and the woman) with power in government were not listening; and street protests were proving ineffectual. The period immediately after the coal strike was particularly depressing. The closure of pits continued, unemployment remained high, trade union membership continued to fall and the outlook for the Valleys was so bleak that the Labour Party and the WTUC preferred not to discuss it.

Then for a brief period the economy revived. Unemployment began to fall and in 1987 Peter Walker surprised Margaret Thatcher by accepting her offer of the Welsh Office and lived up to Hugo Young's assessment of him:

He was very experienced. He knew what he was doing. He had a record of maximising every public position in which he ever found himself. Above all, he was an expert manipulator of the media, having spent a fair amount of his political life attending to the way things would play on the nine o'clock news.[19]

The only survivor of Heathite Conservatism in her Cabinet he brought an invigorating style to the Welsh Office and launched his Valleys Initiative with fanfares of publicity. Under the impact of his daily up-beat press releases, pessimism began to melt away. The irony in this was that Young's assessment of Walker referred to his appointment in 1984 as Secretary of State for Energy, Thatcher's 'ideal candidate to handle a pit strike' – the outcome of which had paved the way for a further rundown of the Valleys communities. Walker was a more expansive personality than his predecessor Nicholas Edwards. His communications with the Wales TUC's general secretary are noticeably warmer in tone and he recognized the Wales TUC as an ally in his attempt to make an impact on the Welsh economy and revive the Valleys. Edwards too had realized that, as we shall see. David Hunt, who followed Walker as Secretary of State, had the same shirt-sleeved style and from his home in the Wirral had considerable knowledge of Wales. With John Redwood the Wales TUC found less rapport, but despite his reputation as an ideologue he was open to argument. In response to pressure from the Wales TUC he introduced a moratorium on competitive tendering while local government in Wales was being reorganized. He reconvened the Welsh Economic Council that Edwards had disbanded. Hague never convened it. Redwood and Hague were more distant than previous Secretaries of State – photo-opportunities with the Wales TUC were not their style – but even so the Wales TUC was always listened to on industrial matters. Throughout those years the expanding powers of the Welsh Office were skilfully exploited by successive Secretaries of State, most of whom looked to play on a bigger stage. The Welsh Office budget that in 1974 had been £1.2 million was by the early 1990s approaching £6 billion.

It was a feature of its relationship with the Welsh Office that the Wales TUC could clearly distinguish and keep separate those areas where there was complete disagreement and those where there was common ground. The same organization that confronted various Secretaries of State over steel closures, the rising level of unemployment and the whole thrust of government policy, often provided positive proposals along with its criticisms. As the trade union voice on the economic problems of Wales it spoke out in all the expected ways, including calls for increased regional aid, the siting of civil service jobs in Wales and a tri-partite economic planning council for Wales. But it also brought to the task an imagination that took unexpected paths. The 1973 'congress' at Llandrindod Wells – part of the campaign to establish the WTUC – received a paper advocating the need for 'a public finance corporation which . . . could monitor investment needs with particular reference to new development and channel funds accordingly'.[20] It was one of the first occasions in Wales that such a call had been made in public, and contributed to the setting up in 1976 of the Welsh Development Agency. It was in that year that the WTUC argued that, rather than supporting the experience of languishing on the dole, the money would be better spent on subsidizing ways of reducing the supply of labour and using spells of unemployment as opportunities for more systematic and targeted training. More fundamental was its active engagement in the provision of jobs in Wales through its support for inward investment and its resource centre for co-operatives. Both these initiatives took it beyond the confines of collective bargaining and government lobbying and into unconventional territory for British trade unionism. They were also two of the few positive moves to come from the demoralized Welsh labour movement in the 1980s.

THE WALES CO-OPERATIVE CENTRE

The idea for a 'Resource Centre' came out of the redundancies of the 1970s. 'Delegations were coming to us and asking for help: we realized that there was no structure in the unions or at the WTUC to provide a service to them.'[21] Attempts were made to help redundant workers from Shotton and East Moors, Homerton Rubber in Treforest and Taff Products, the co-operative spin-off from the closure of Triang Toys, Merthyr Tydfil. But as the number of redundancies increased in 1979–80 it became clear that a formal structure was needed. The 1970s had been a time of considerable debate about industrial democracy, workers' control and the value of extending power and opportunity to workers through producer co-operatives.[22] The Labour government established in 1978 the Co-operative Development Agency. The West Midlands County Council and the Greater London Enterprise Board were both promoting co-operative enterprises. Why should not the Wales TUC play a part in supporting worker co-operatives? The notion was first set out in the document *Wales at the Abyss* submitted to the Social Affairs and Employment Committee of the European Parliament on 21 February 1980.

The Wales TUC intends to set up a new organisation – the Resource Centre – to combat the blight of unemployment and accelerated industrial decline . . . The proposed Resource Centre intends to draw on the professional, technical and financial resources available from those directly affected by this latest wave of plant closures and redundancies.[23]

The successful producer co-operatives established at the Basque town of Mondragon were proposed as a possible model. Similar evidence was presented to the Committee on Welsh Affairs in April. This bold intention, written into the document at the last moment by Dennis Gregory, needed flesh put upon it. In August the Welsh Office was asked for a grant to investigate the feasibility of providing assistance to potential co-operatives. How could a request designed to generate jobs from within Wales be refused? In November £40,000 was made available, subsequently supplemented by £5,000 from the Welsh Development Agency.

The investigators were Denis Gregory and Chris Logan a senior consultant with Logica Ltd. Logan was already familiar with the Basque country and its language for his mother was Basque, and he had co-authored a book about the Mondragon co-operatives.[24] It was while he was working as a consultant on feasibility studies for the regeneration of Shotton, Ebbw Vale and East Moors that the WTUC researchers Gregory and Atkinson had first made contact with him, and he planted the co-operative idea with Gregory. Together they held meetings and seminars with trade unionists, studied six workers' co-ops in Wales, examined forms of co-operation in the United States, assessed the trade union involvement in the co-operative sector of the Italian economy and, with a delegation from the WTUC, looked in depth at the banking and professional services supplied by the Caja Laboral Popular in Mondragon. All who went to Mondragon came back total converts and the publicity aroused was priceless. A television crew from Granada's *World in Action* followed them around all week, as did Vincent Kane and a team from BBC Wales. A video of the visit was shown again and again in labour movement meetings throughout Wales. The report concluded that, across a range of economic sectors, co-operatives were a feasible form of enterprise. To make this happen in Wales there should be established a resource centre to provide training in the necessary professional and managerial skills, and an investment fund dedicated to the provision of risk capital for new co-operatives.[25]

Despite this report, published in September 1981, and the enthusiastic response given to it by local authorities and endorsement by the WTUC conferences in 1982 and 1983, progress remained slow. In the summer of 1982 an approach to Ivor Richard, the EEC Commissioner for Employment and Social Affairs, resulted in the EEC agreeing to match any funds provided by the Welsh Office to set up the resource centre. In the end the Welsh Office provided £100,000 for three years, the European Social Fund £60,000 for the first year, 1983, followed by £97,600 for 1984, the Welsh Development Agency provided £45,000 for three years and the Development Board for Rural Wales £5,000 for three years. In addition, the majority of county councils contributed £10,000 per annum and district and town councils contributed on average £2,500 per annum.[26] Thereafter, a succession of grants from the EEC, the WDA and the DBRW ensured the resource centre's future. South Glamorgan County Council provided premises for the centre at Llandaff Court and George Wright launched it at the Sherman Theatre, Cardiff, on 15 April 1983. Les Paul, the treasurer of the WTUC, was in this as in other ventures an enthusiastic and tireless supporter. But the idea for an investment fund, initially backed by the Co-operative Bank, turned out to be not legally feasible, and never came to fruition.

Today the Wales Co-operative Centre is the largest co-operative development agency in the UK. David Jenkins recalls that 'it was George's baby. He drove it through against all difficulties' and Wright himself says: 'It was two-and-a-half years of head down graft to bring it into being. It was a belief thing.' He personally visited almost every local authority in Wales to raise funds for the centre. The TUC's initial reaction was that it was not something that the TUC did and that it should not be pursued. 'It's not our role' said Len Murray, but later the TUC warmed to the idea and in 1985 published a supportive statement and guidelines on workers' co-operatives.[27] Some public sector unions in Wales saw it as a diversion of resources from the struggle against privatization. The majority were 'agnostic' – willing to support it in conference resolutions but seeing it as a marginal activity. Nonetheless, in the depression of the early 1980s unions increasingly referred groups of their members to the centre for advice and assistance in creating employment opportunities. In 1983 the number of co-operatives either registered or trading in Wales was twenty-eight employing the equivalent of 140 full-time workers. By 1987 there were ninety-five co-operatives employing 643 equivalents.[28] The centre was firmly established.

Over the years its activities have developed from dealing solely with producer co-operatives to supporting credit unions, marketing co-operatives, community co-operatives, and employee buy-outs,

including the one at Tower Colliery. More than 200 co-operative
businesses in Wales have been established, providing work and training
for thousands of people. Long before it was fashionable to speak of the
social economy, or of creating an entrepreneurial Wales, the Wales TUC
took practical steps to encourage indigenous growth and for over twenty
years has made through the centre a modest, but distinctive, contribution to Welsh economic development.

INWARD INVESTMENT

The engagement with inward investment came earlier. Its origin lay in
the ferment of ideas and activity that surrounded the birth of the Wales
TUC and the Labour victory of 1974, the economic challenge of the
European Community, the conception of the Welsh Development
Agency, and the continuing haemorrhage of jobs from coal and steel. For
George Wright, the powerful new voice in Welsh politics, the priorities
were clear. Wales needed jobs. There should be one organization – the
WDA – to promote investment. The trade unions had to have a role in
the process.

> The Wales TUC was about jobs and looking after the community. The old
> regional policy of carrots and sticks had brought work to Wales but we needed
> companies that *wanted* to come here. For me there was a positive message that
> we could portray about Wales and the unions. I liked doing that.[29]

Wright was asked by John Morris, the Secretary of State, and by the
Invest in Britain Bureau of the Department of Trade and Industry, to
present his positive vision to potential investors.

The very act of persuading foreign investors to site their factories in
Wales was objectionable to some. Despite rising unemployment, there
was considerable suspicion about the investment activities of multi-
national corporations. The TUC Congress in 1975 carried a resolution
drawing attention to 'the threat to democratic processes caused by the
increasing proportion of industry owned by multi-national companies'.
But for the Wales TUC inward investment was a provider of jobs, a way
of diversifying the economy, and a more realizable alternative than the
TUC policy of selective import controls. At the Economic and Industrial
Committee on 28 September 1978 a discussion took place

during which the attention of the committee was drawn to certain criticisms that had been made of the policy of the Wales TUC to openly encourage inward investment.

The Committee felt however that it was far preferable to have foreign companies manufacturing in Wales rather than them importing the finished product into the Principality. It was subsequently agreed: That the present policy of the Wales TUC, of assisting and co-operating with any company wishing to invest in Wales, is seen as the best way of ensuring that such investment is to the ultimate benefit of its members.[30]

The government's attitude was clarified by Alan Williams, MP for Swansea West and Minister of State at the Department of Industry, in responding to the secretary of Swansea 10 branch of the AUEW who had written expressing concern about Japanese companies setting up in Wales.

This government welcomes and encourages inward investment . . . Unless we take a very positive attitude to Japanese investment, wherever the national interest will be served, we may well have to face their competition from within the [European] Community . . .

The government has been grateful to George Wright for the support he has given us in obtaining Japanese investment.[31]

Of course, foreign investment in the Welsh economy long pre-dated the formation of the Wales TUC. It began in earnest in the 1960s. In 1958 there were fewer than thirty foreign manufacturing firms in Wales employing some 15,000 people, but by the end of 1979 there were 177 employing over 55,000 people. Even in the mid-1970s the number of people employed by foreign firms exceeded the number employed in coalmining. More than half the firms were American, with another third coming from Europe. The first Japanese manufacturing company did not come to Wales until 1972.[32] It cannot be argued, therefore, that the Wales TUC played a defining role in bringing foreign investors to Wales. The availability of labour, grants and financial assistance, office and factory space, and good communications were more significant.[33] But it played a part that was by no means insignificant. From the mid-1970s George Wright travelled extensively to meet foreign industrialists and persuade them of the skills and virtues of Welsh labour and the peaceful character of industrial relations in Wales.

The initial coolness between the WTUC and the Welsh Office that came with the change of government in 1979 was gradually replaced by a recognition that in the area of economic development, at least, there was a mutual interest. Although seen as being on the right wing of the Cabinet, Edwards was a Welshman who cared deeply about Wales and no Secretary of State could ignore the massive increases in unemployment that followed the 1979 election. From around 6 per cent in 1978, unemployment in Wales rose to over 15 per cent in 1984. Out of that the Tory Welsh Office and the Wales TUC found common ground.

> We stumbled upon areas of agreement – regional policy, inward investment, indigenous growth – where the Welsh Office could deliver better with the help of the Wales TUC. The Welsh Office and the Wales TUC were lined up on regional policy versus the Department of Trade and Industry.[34]

It was the Wales TUC that took the initiative. At a meeting on 4 June 1980 George Wright proposed that the Wales TUC and the CBI Wales should jointly with the Welsh Office set up an Industrial Relations Promotion Unit. Its purpose would be to explain to potential inward investors that industrial relations in the UK were better than painted in the media, and that the record in Wales was better still. Its primary function would be 'the propagation and promotion of Wales as an area of industrial expansion'. The Secretary of State received this idea 'with interest' and, whilst eventually it was decided that such a unit was not feasible, it was agreed that on all major trade missions a Wales TUC representative would be present.[35] In 1981 the WTUC chairman, John Griffiths, accompanied the Secretary of State to the United States and Japan. The escalating level of unemployment and the necessity to replace jobs lost in coal and steel gave efforts to find inward investors a new urgency. Despite continuing disagreements with the government over the treatment of the coal and steel industries, the WTUC was a willing collaborator in this. One example from many at that time illustrates the point. On 2 February 1981 George Wright wrote to Nicholas Edwards concerning the possibility of a major Nissan plant being located in Wales. 'It cannot be stressed too strongly that the Wales TUC wishes to co-operate with the Welsh Office and its various agencies in ensuring that this investment is secured for the Principality and in ensuring its future success and viability.' In response, Edwards's private secretary wrote, 'The Secretary of State has asked me to say that it is helpful to have this firm confirmation of the desire of the Wales TUC to co-operate fully in ensuring the success of the Nissan project if it is located in Wales.'[36]

It became a regular practice for members of the general council of the Wales TUC to accompany trade missions overseas to woo inward investors and in 1984 the Secretary of State invited David Jenkins, the new Wales TUC general secretary, to accompany him on a mission to Japan. For some in the labour movement it was inconceivable that the WTUC was collaborating with a government that was legislating to curb union activities.[37] Others, including the TUC and the Scottish TUC, were envious of the way it managed to retain some influence whilst combating unemployment. The 'growth coalition' comprising the WDA, CBI Wales, local authorities, the Welsh Office and the Wales TUC had undoubted success. Between 1982 and 1992 Wales secured proportionately more investment projects and jobs than any other region of the UK. By 1993 the number of overseas-owned production units had risen to 348 employing 68,000 people, over 30 per cent of total Welsh manufacturing employment.

SINGLE-UNION AGREEMENTS

There was another aspect to the support given by the Wales TUC to direct foreign investment that aroused criticism. Inward investment meant jobs, and jobs meant potential union members. But jobs at what price; and members at what price? The criticism arose from the procedures adopted to gain union members in these new firms, frequently before a single worker had been employed.

From the beginning, trade union leaders in Wales realized that the growth of inward investment from American and European companies presented a new challenge to unions. Most investors came from countries where union membership was weak and unions barely tolerated, whereas membership levels in Wales were high compared even to the UK average. Consequently the WTUC lost no opportunity to stress to the Welsh Office and the CBI that trade union recognition should be part of any discussions with firms wishing to site in Wales.[38] Through the contacts developed on trade missions and advisory approaches made to incoming firms, the Wales TUC, along with CBI Wales, came to be accepted by the Welsh Office, local authorities and Welsh Development Agency as a referral point for firms wishing to understand the realities of industrial relations in Wales.

In a paper written for the general council in 1987 David Jenkins, as general secretary of the Wales TUC set out how the system had worked for many years. Upon receiving a referral the general secretary of the WTUC met representatives of the in-coming company and explained to them the advantages of recognizing at the very beginning the appropriate unions. He would point out that to operate without any agreement could be both difficult and hazardous, given the high level of unionization in Wales. Difficult because many of the workforce would in any event be trade union members; hazardous because experience showed that sooner or later the company would be faced with competing claims by different unions, all claiming by then to represent some part of the labour force. Companies that had followed WTUC advice enjoyed excellent industrial relations and the in-coming company was advised to recognize the contribution of strong trade union organization to achieving this. It would be extremely sensible therefore to discuss recognition with all unions appropriate to the company's business. At that stage the company would either show no interest in union recognition, or take up the WTUC offer to arrange meetings with appropriate unions, or make its own independent approaches to one or more unions for detailed discussions.

Complementary to this procedure and providing an essential underpinning was an accord between the major unions in Wales. It was agreed that all relevant unions would have an opportunity to put their case to an in-coming company but, once a company had agreed to recognize a union or unions prior to taking on staff, then the unsuccessful unions would withdraw, leaving the field to the successful one(s). This accord was crucial in sustaining the advocacy of the Wales TUC office. The fact that it did not apply where a company belatedly realized the need for union recognition was a central plank of the case advanced by the Wales TUC office. In such circumstances, it was pointed out, a number of unions could establish competing membership rights. The virtue of the accord was that normally competitive unions cooperated in an orderly process of unionization. 'The fear of many companies from outside the UK of being faced with a myriad of differing claims from many different unions is thereby effectively and properly exorcised.'[39]

In fact, the great majority of recognition agreements were made with one union, although not always the same one. Initially these single-union deals were promoted to its member firms by the Engineering Employers' Association in Wales and by George Wright who had seen in the Midlands the complexities and jealousies aroused by having numerous unions in the same factory. Two further steps reinforced single-union recognition agreements: 'the check-off' – a system whereby union dues were subtracted from the worker's pay by the employer on behalf of the union – and the 'closed shop' where all workers were required to join the relevant union as a condition of employment. Japanese companies in particular desired single-union agreements, as they were accustomed in Japan to dealing with unions confined to a single enterprise. Single-union deals were not new. Across manufacturing industry as a whole in the early 1980s more than half the workplaces recognized only one manual workers' union, and almost two-thirds recognized only one white-collar union.[40] It was rare, however, for one union to represent all grades of workers. One of the earliest in Welsh manufacturing industry came in 1973 when Sony signed a deal with the Amalgamated Union of Engineering Workers (AUEW). When Mr Aso of the Japanese Embassy met a Wales TUC representative in 1981 he was assured that single-union agreements were already in operation in many industries in Wales, and especially in a number of Japanese companies.

> If Japanese companies wished to apply single Union Agreements, then following discussions by a company, and whichever trade union, agreement could be made which could include sole negotiating and recognition rights, and also agreement on a Closed Shop which would be distinctly advantageous to both Company and Union. Agreements of this kind once completed, would be recognised by every other Trade Union.[41]

NEW-STYLE AGREEMENTS

The most dramatic event for a trade union movement in decline in the 1980s was the miners' strike. It marked the end for the foreseeable future of that militancy which characterized British unions in the 1960s and 1970s. But even while it was taking place a 'new industrial relations' appeared to be emerging in Wales. If the role of the Wales TUC in the miners' strike was marginal, its involvement in a new approach to industrial relations was central. It was also controversial.

The criticisms were extensive and not always accurate. Briefly they were as follows. By indiscriminately welcoming jobs at any price the Wales TUC collaborated in producing a low-paid, de-skilled labour force, where women filled part-time jobs and men remained unemployed. By promoting 'beauty parades' where unions offered their services to employers inter-union competition was encouraged, employers dictated the nature of agreements and decided which union workers would join, and 'no strike' deals denied to workers and unions the ultimate sanction of industrial action. Moreover, the WTUC allowed itself to be incorporated into a Tory policy dictated by the Welsh Office.

The criticisms really focus on two areas: the involvement in persuading inward investors to site in Wales; and the nature of subsequent recognition agreements. On the first point it is well to recall that unemployment, steadily increasing in the 1970s, had become the most serious social issue of the 1980s, when it was on a scale comparable to the 1930s. When thousands of jobs were being lost, not just in coal and steel but also in manufacturing, it made sense at the regional level to woo new employers. Inward investment was not an alien imposition but an alternative to the dole and empty factory buildings, and as such warmly welcomed by workers and their communities. It is true that many of the jobs were part-time and for women. It is also true that Wales entered the 1980s near the top of the earnings league and was near the bottom on entering the 1990s. But that reflected the loss of jobs in coal, chemicals and steel, on the one hand, and on the other, the work that was available – high-volume routine assembly operations. If better paid jobs had been on offer they would have been taken. No one was offering to open coalmines or start up new steel mills. It is also true that many of the new jobs were semi-skilled assembly work. The fact that these were appropriate to the labour skills available is not a comment upon the trade unions but upon the insufficient diversification of the economy, and the failure of past employers to invest in technology and people. Even so, the picture was not as bad as has been painted. The rate of growth of managers and professional engineers employed in the electronics and motor components industries was well above the UK average in the twelve years to 1990.[42]

The wooing of inward investors was a pragmatic response to a real problem and the policy of both political parties when in office. Nor was the Wales TUC 'incorporated' in the sense that it exercised restraint in certain areas in return for advantageous concessions from the government of the day. No concessions were made and its criticisms of government policy on steel and coal closures, on the National Health Service and general economic policy were loud and emphatic. But there is no doubt that in the restricted area of inward investment a form of 'social partnership' was practised in Wales. With Mrs Thatcher in Downing Street, the Secretary of State for Wales sat on platforms in Japan and the USA and introduced a Welsh trade unionist as part of his 'team'. It was unique. In no other region of Britain was there a comparable alliance.

It had its roots in two areas of Welsh life. The first is a labour movement tradition of practical action rather than theoretical debate. That tradition is represented by eighty years of Labour-dominated councils using their powers to achieve a more humane and civilized society. It is complemented by a trade unionism that calls for more wages rather than the end of the wage system; that exists as a form of resistance to capitalism, yet accepts the need to work within it to achieve a better life for people here and now. Sometimes called 'Labourism' it has been the creed of the mainstream of the British labour movement.

The second area was Welsh identity. 'One of the strengths of Wales is a common bond. Your starting point is that you are not *them* – England.'[43] From that common identity comes a shared understanding, a mutually acceptable ideology that is again practical in content: the defence and promotion of Wales. In the context of the staggering job losses in the late 1970s and early 1980s, that meant focusing on the economy. The fact that Wales is a small country where networks are easy to forge and the members of the political class know practically every one else in the arena reinforced the move to social partnership. Credit must be given too to successive Secretaries of State who recognized the opportunities and seized them. To complete the picture, the devolved Welsh Office and the Wales TUC provided the institutional framework to bring the actors together. Out of that belief in 'Wales plc' came the 'growth coalition'.

The other main criticism concerns the nature of agreements made between inward investors and trade unions. 'Beauty parades' – a term not used in the Wales TUC – were a highly successful method of *controlling* inter-union competition over recruitment. Moreover, it was an open process understood and accepted by all concerned. Only when the system broke down in the mid-1980s did problems begin (see Chapter 5). It is true that on greenfield sites union agreements were reached before anyone had been employed. 'But it was either that or no union at all. We brought employers in, and unionized them. Remember, in the Thatcher and Major years employers were encouraged to derecognize trade unions. There wasn't much of that in Wales.'[44]

The evidence supports this view. Only three of twenty-seven electronics plants surveyed in the early 1980s were non-union. A decade later, a survey of twenty-four 'Japanese transplants in Wales' found that only two were non-unionized, while the density of union membership in the plants was considerably higher than that for Japanese companies in the rest of the UK.[45] This contrasts strongly with what happened in West Lothian where Japanese electronics manufacturers refused to recognize even the EETPU.[46] Contrary to the view that the Wales TUC and unions in Wales totally surrendered to the demands of inward investors, the incomers – not just the Japanese – had to come to terms with the culture of trade unionism that the Wales TUC impressed upon them.

Certainly these agreements were a two-way street. With mass unemployment and a political climate favouring 'macho management', in-coming investors had the power to insist on a certain kind of single-union deal. It was a package that shifted the frontier of control at the point of production away from shop stewards and towards management. Agreements acknowledged the right of management to deploy labour as it saw fit, to communicate to employees directly on any matter deemed appropriate and spelled out the necessity for continuity of production. The package also contained benefits for individual workers that British unions had often advocated and British employers resisted – equal status, sick pay and holiday entitlements, medical check-ups, training and a more open management style. Not all single-union deals included 'no strike' clauses, although a majority of those signed by Japanese companies with the EETPU did. However, whilst such clauses were at the centre of considerable controversy in the 1980s, they were of limited significance. In the last resort they were no more than statements of intent. There was no legally binding agreement not to strike and workers were always free to take unconstitutional or unofficial industrial action, and did so in a number of cases. Secondly, strikes have nearly always been weapons of last resort, with many unions, particularly those with weak bargaining power, preferring arbitration. Also, as employers realized that arbitration could well impede their exercise of prerogatives, it became rarely used.[47] The deals that were signed were not ideal from a trade union point of view. But the Wales TUC and individual unions were not in a position to impose their wishes. In a review of developments across Britain in the 1980s an experienced and well-informed observer commented:

> It is hard to avoid the conclusion that the structure of trade unionism, originally developed for the strategies of employee solidarity, is increasingly being shaped to the needs of employers . . . this co-operation may be the only means of preventing the expansion of non-union employer practices . . . The employer's control of recognition has always been a crucial determinant of union development.[48]

In the labour and product market conditions of the 1980s inward investors, without agreeing to recognize trade unions, could have unilaterally imposed their requirements upon workers grateful for a job. This was in fact what employers were doing throughout much of manufacturing industry across the rest of the UK.

The election of Mrs Thatcher precipitated a crisis of trade unionism that has continued into the twenty-first century. Throughout that time the Wales TUC promoted indigenous enterprise and supported inward investment, always with the recruitment of trade union members in mind. The outcomes were not always ideal. But trade union practices have never been cast in stone. They are the outcome of historical circumstances and in particular the existing power relations between capital and labour at any one time. In the 1980s and much of the 1990s it was a case of adapting to a hostile environment and keeping the principles of collectivism alive for another and better day.

Chapter 5

New Directions

Times change, and we change with them. (Anonymous)

As the delegates assembled in Llandudno for the Wales TUC conference in May 1984 the miners were on strike; a new and full-time general secretary – David Jenkins – was about to take his first conference; and George Wright was in the thick of an election campaign to succeed Moss Evans as the next general secretary of the TGWU, then the largest union in the United Kingdom. With 507 branches backing him, compared with 397 for the other leading contender Ron Todd, Wright's hopes were high. He did not win: but the election exposed a ballot-rigging scandal – centred mainly but not exclusively on the union's Irish region – which caused the election to be run again in 1985. On both occasions Wright finished as runner-up. For eighteen months he campaigned for the biggest prize in the trade union world and it eluded him. For ten years he had served as general secretary of the Wales TUC but that too had ended. In 1991 he once again contested the top job in the TGWU but without success. As regional secretary of the TGWU he continued to be a dominating personality in Welsh trade union and internal Labour Party affairs but the direction of the Wales TUC had now passed to other hands.

A NEW GENERAL SECRETARY

David Jenkins the new full-time general secretary came from a very different background from Wright's. Born and raised in Cardiff, the son of a semi-skilled manual worker, he attended Cantonian High School before going to Liverpool University where he graduated in politics and economics in 1970. Left-wing in politics, he was president of the university's Socialist Society, 'the rag-tag of the far left'. He believed trade unions to be the vehicle for radical change in society, confronting capitalism on the front line. He applied for a job with the TUC after leaving university but was told to get work experience. He joined ITT Distributors in Cardiff, a firm dealing in electrical components, as a buyer and industrial sales organizer but left over a difference in policy: 'I thought there was too much emphasis on the profit drive and that customers were not getting the service they deserved.' He then worked for a year at GKN steelworks, Cardiff, driving heavy lifting machinery, before taking a teacher training course and securing a post as a lecturer in liberal studies at Peterborough Technical College. He rapidly became secretary of the local branch of the National Association of Teachers in Further and Higher Education (NATFHE) and then secretary for the whole Cambridge and district area. Union work soon displaced his teaching duties and, as he became less and less the lecturer and more and more the trade union organizer, Jenkins felt at home. 'I knew that my original instinct to work with trade unions was right.' After two-and-a-half years he saw the post of administrator/researcher for the Wales TUC advertised. The TUC had agreed to fund the post after representations by the WTUC that its research grant was coming to an end and that developing commitments were outstripping its administrative capabilities. Jenkins applied, and was successful. The appointment, made by the TUC in 1978, was the first full-time post in the TUC's regional structure.

For Jenkins it was a watershed. 'Coming to the Wales TUC fundamentally changed my understanding of trade unions.' Dealing with day-to-day problems made him realize that, regardless of theoretical debates, 'people join trade unions for immediate answers to immediate problems. Trade unions are not there to change society but to provide practical support within the existing environment. I therefore take a pragmatic line. It's more productive.'

In September 1983 he was appointed full-time general secretary and until May 1984, when George Wright stepped down, they worked in tandem. The Wales TUC had moved with the TGWU from Charles Street into the new Cathedral Road building opened by Jim Callaghan in 1979. Jenkins's early years in the WTUC brought him to realize that, despite excellent research reports from Gregory and Atkinson and superb handling of the media by Wright, there was little substance to the organization. A structure was needed to support the head. The committees below the general council were built up and their discussions fed into the decision-making process. Bureaucracy was added to flair. Differences in style were inevitable. Wright was regional secretary of the most powerful union in Wales with a sense of power and how to use it. Jenkins was an employee of the TUC and, like all executives, had to be aware of the power blocs on his general council. Wright was the leader of the major power bloc and had not exhausted his ambition. Jenkins did not have the additional task of running the Wales region of the TGWU. He made it his business to cultivate ministers, civil servants and members of quangos.[1]

It was not a good time to become general secretary of the Wales TUC. The ferment of the pioneering days was over; the miners were engaged in a bitter dispute that had split both the union and the trade union movement; more than a decade of trade union political marginalization lay ahead; and trade union membership was in free fall. In Wales the decline in membership was as much qualitative as quantitative. The seismic upheaval in the job market had dramatically altered the composition of the working population and taken away the foundations of traditional working-class culture. When more worked in banks than in the pits, it was the end of Wales as most people understood it. By the late 1980s competition between unions in Wales would precipitate a major crisis within the TUC. Confined to the margins of political influence, the TUC and WTUC became inward-looking, as did their affiliated unions. Confronted by a confident Welsh Office and a proliferation of quangos[2] the Wales TUC, always under-resourced, sought more freedom from the TUC. But the greatest challenge to the unions throughout these years was the continuing loss of membership.

THE HAEMORRHAGE OF MEMBERS

Each year from 1980 to 1998 trade union membership fell, the longest continuous decline on record. It was a massive loss not just of membership, but also of finances and influence. The number of trade unionists in unions affiliated to the Wales TUC fell by a quarter: from 649,000 in 1979 to 484,900 in 2002. That still leaves 40 per cent of Welsh employees in a union compared with only 30 per cent in Great Britain as a whole, where trade union membership fell from 12.6 million in 1979 to 7.3 million in 2003.

The causes of union decline are well known. Unemployment certainly played a major part in initiating the decline, taking large numbers out of the labour force in the early 1980s and 1990s and providing a continuing backdrop of fear that inhibited organization. As Emlyn Williams told the NUM south Wales area annual conference in May 1983: 'To put it bluntly. Unemployment takes the guts out of people.' The proportion of the labour force unemployed in Wales doubled between 1980 and 1986, moving from 6.9 to 13.9 per cent, representing 166,000 people (excluding school leavers) 'on the dole'. Thereafter the proportion declined, but only once in the years up to 1997 – in 1990 – did it return to the 1980 level. For most of the time it remained above 9 per cent. In 1995 when the percentage of the labour force claiming unemployment benefit stood at 8.5 per cent, this still represented 107,000 people. As the method of calculating unemployment was changed over thirty times between 1979 and 1995, almost every time reducing the figure, the real number was many more. Nor did unemployment strike men and women equally. Throughout the 1980s and 1990s more than 70 per cent of the unemployed were men. And for most of the period almost a third of all unemployed were in the age group 18–24.[3]

The level of unemployment among young people meant that a generation grew up in Wales without any contact with trade unionism. Side by side with unemployment went the restructuring, indeed the deindustrialization, of the economy that broke up the concentrations of highly unionized workers in coal, steel, chemicals, printing, textiles, docks and engineering. As early as 1968, manufacturing in south Wales was providing nearly twice as many jobs as coal steel and tinplate combined and the service sector was providing more than three times as many. Even on the coalfield there were more jobs in services than in coalmining. Manufacturing continued to grow until 1974 and the service sector expanded throughout the 1970s so that by 1979, for Wales as a whole, manufacturing provided more than seven-and-a-half times as many jobs as there were in coal, and services provided *fifteen* times as many. But there came a dramatic collapse in manufacturing employment between 1979 and 1983 when Wales lost more manufacturing jobs (relative to population) than any other area of Britain.[4] Manufacturing employment since then has continued to decline in Wales and throughout Britain while service jobs grow apace. The decline in manufacturing would probably be greater but for the number of jobs created by foreign inward investment over the period. In 2000 foreign-owned companies employed approximately 6 per cent of the employed workforce in Wales, and 36 per cent of employees in manufacturing. Most of these jobs were in industries like electronics, motor vehicle components and chemicals that had high growth rates in productivity. In addition, many more jobs were created in firms supplying these incomers. The distribution of these jobs however is highly concentrated, with three-quarters of the plants in the north-east and south-east areas of the country.[5]

The Welsh economy has therefore been completely transformed during the lifetime of the Wales TUC. The employment figures in Table 1 illustrate what has happened. Jobs in the agricultural sector, which includes forestry and fishing, halved over the period 1975–2001. The energy sector – that includes mining, electricity, gas and water supply – has 55,000 fewer workers. (The number of coalminers fell from 38,000 to 2,000.) Manufacturing has 128,000 fewer workers and services 284,000 more. In brief, the energy sector has lost 90 per cent of its jobs, the manufacturing sector 40 per cent, and three-quarters of all Welsh employees now work in the service sector. Wales is increasingly a post-industrial society. The state, however, continues to be a major employer providing, through public administration, health and education alone, jobs for almost a third of Welsh workers. The comparable figure for Britain is just under a quarter.

Table 1. Employment in Wales by sector ('000s)

	1975	1989	2001
Agriculture	26	21	13
Energy	62	29	7
Manufacturing	317	250	189
Construction	66	43	57
Services	527	647	811
Total employees	998	979	1,077
Total males	620	517	504
Total females	378	462	574

Source: Contemporary Wales. The figures are estimates and provided solely to illustrate broad sectoral changes.

To these economic factors were added further features unfavourable to trade unionism – the privatization of publicly owned industries, the increase in small workplaces and self-employment, the growth of part-time and contract work, legislation that strengthened employer sanctions against unions, state attitudes (not least the determined defeat of the miners in 1985) and management techniques embodied in 'human resource management'. It was a cumulative process, leading to the non-recognition of unions and even their de-recognition. There was a 10 per cent decline in union recognition for manual employees in Welsh private industry between 1980 and 1990, although that was only half the fall experienced in other regions. For non-manual employees the drop was higher but still five percentage points below the UK average.[6] By the late 1980s employers had discovered that they did not *have* to recognize trade unions. In David Jenkins's opinion: 'The habit of recognizing unions has gone.'

The other significant feature of Table 1 is that women now clearly outnumber men in employment. Since 1974 almost one man in every five has disappeared from the labour force, while female employment has increased by over 50 per cent. Historically, because women were largely excluded from the traditional industries of coal, steel and quarrying, only a small proportion were recorded as economically active, although official records probably understated the true extent of women's paid work. The 1961 census indicated that 'three-quarters of women in Wales did *not* have any paid work outside the home'.[7] During the 1960s and 1970s the number of women in employment increased rapidly as the new manufacturing and service employments enthusiastically recruited this untapped source of labour. Female employment in manufacturing fell back during the recession of the early 1980s but the really significant sector was services, where eight out of ten women now work. The proportion of women in the labour force accelerated from 33 per cent in 1972, to 38 per cent in 1980, to more than 50 per cent today. But with that increase there has been a sharp rise in the number of women working part-time. By 2001, 54 per cent of all women employees in Wales were part-time. Many, often married women, work in medical services and retail distribution where flexible working is prevalent, as it is in call centres.

At first, in trying to come to terms with the blitzkreig that hit them, trade union leaders concentrated on tactics of basic survival. One line of approach was to provide members with services such as discounts on cars, favourable mortgage rates, low insurance premiums and shopping discounts. It was argued that unions needed to forge a new relationship with each individual member, rather like the successful and rapidly growing Automobile Association.[8]

Another basic response as members drained away was to merge with another union – sometimes, not always, consolidating the members in certain industries but usually achieving financial savings. Between 1980 and 1991 there were 149 mergers and amalgamations involving 4.25 million workers. The process continued into the 1990s. Among the more notable mergers were the following. The TGWU absorbed the textile and agricultural workers in 1982, and the GMWU amalgamated with the Boilermakers in the same year to become the GMBATU. Subsequently it absorbed a dozen unions in the garment and textile industries, changed its name to GMB in 1987 and amalgamated with APEX in 1989. The white-collar unions TASS and ASTMS merged to form MSF in 1988; the seamen and railwaymen merged in 1990 and became the RMT; the broadcasting unions merged in 1991; the major post office unions merged into the CWU; the major print unions became the GPMU in 1992 and that same year the engineers and the electricians merged to become the AEEU; three large public sector unions joined together to form Unison in 1993 and in 2001 MSF and the AEEU merged to become AMICUS. These mergers have considerably altered, although not simplified, the structure of British trade unionism. The chief numerical effect has been to reduce the total number of unions and partially mitigate the loss of members in some unions.[9] The consequences for major unions in Wales can be seen in Table 2.

Table 2. Membership of ten largest unions affiliated to the WTUC

1974		2003	
Union	Membership	Union	Membership
TGWU	115,000	AMICUS	103,410
AUEW (Eng.)	75,650	Unison	90,148
NUGMW	48,000	TGWU	65,473
NUM	42,000	GMB	51,000
ISTC	39,500	PCS	21,000
NALGO	33,750	USDAW	21,000
EETPU	30,000	CWU	16,300
NUPE	29,700	NUT	16,150
NUT	17,700	NASUWT	15,500
USDAW	16,700	NUM	12,000

Source: Wales TUC Annual Reports.

The number of unions affiliated to the WTUC fell from sixty-eight in 1974 to fifty-three in 2003 and the membership is now much more concentrated. The four largest unions in 1974 had 45 per cent of total Wales TUC membership; in 2003 they had 63 per cent. Non-manual workers predominate. In addition to the local and national government workers within Unison (inherited from NALGO), and the substantial white-collar section within AMICUS, there are two teachers' unions in the 2003 top ten, together with the PCS, the largest civil service union.

Although steelworks closures have removed the ISTC from the top ten (in 2003 it was eleventh with 9,552 members), the NUM remains there despite the virtual extinction of deep mining. That is because retired miners can remain in membership and it has five times as many retired members as there are working miners. But the other unions also include retired members in their membership figures. As there is no external check upon the numbers they affiliate to the Wales TUC all these membership figures need therefore to be taken with a large pinch of salt. Nonetheless, Labour Force Surveys confirm that Wales with, in 2002, 40 per cent of employees unionized remains the most unionized part of Great Britain, the average for which is 29 per cent. By international standards the strength of trade unionism in Wales is high.

A BITTER CONFLICT

In the scramble for membership in the 1980s the authority that the Wales TUC had exerted over its affiliated unions in relation to recruitment and inward investment broke down. A WTUC initiative to increase recruitment in mid-Wales, following conference motions, did not get off the ground in August 1989 as the unions concerned would not divulge membership figures in the area to the WTUC. They were four of its most important affiliates – the TGWU, MSF, AEU and GMB.

The reasons for the loss of authority were several. The marginalization of the Wales TUC by the Welsh Office weakened its standing with affiliated unions. The Employment Acts of 1980 and 1982 began to erode the closed shop, a bulwark of single-union deals. The 1988 and 1992 Acts undermined it completely, making it unfair to dismiss a worker for non-membership of a union, or to refuse employment to anyone who was not a member of a union. As membership numbers fell, competition between unions grew and they began to make direct approaches for recognition to potential inward investors. The EETPU in particular was uninhibited in pursuing its own interests. Unlike most of the other unions, it openly declared its commitment to single-union deals and to 'no strike' agreements. It had pioneered them at the Toshiba factory in Plymouth in 1981. Its presentations to employers were professional; its glossy fourteen-page prospectus emphasized the quality and breadth of technical skills offered at its training centre at Cudham Hall (opened by Norman Tebbit in 1985); and it sent senior officials to Japan to sell the union to prospective investors.[10] As the number of Japanese firms in

Wales rapidly increased, from just four in the 1970s to over twenty by 1989, the established ones advised in-coming compatriots about the unions most amenable to their demands. More so than American companies, they were willing to grant recognition to a trade union, but increasingly it was on *their* terms.

In 1982 the GMB union, acting within the WTUC/union accord, signed a single-union deal with the Aiwa company at Blackwood. For the first time in Wales the agreement contained a 'no strike' clause as part of the recognition agreement, both sides agreeing to accept an arbitrator's decision in cases of dispute. In 1983, again following WTUC procedures, a single-union deal including binding arbitration was agreed between the EETPU and Inmos, a state-funded microchip company at Newport. In the same year the EETPU achieved a similar deal with AB Electronics at Rogerstone. None of these deals caught public attention. What happened next changed all that.

In 1984 the former GEC/Hitachi television and video plant at Hirwaun became wholly owned by Hitachi and the company signed a single-union 'no strike' agreement with the EETPU. Five unions – the AUEW, UCATT, ASTMS, APEX and TASS – that had been recognized by the previous owners were thereby excluded. The five, together with the TGWU, took the EETPU to the TUC disputes committee on the grounds that the agreement would deprive them of their existing recognition and negotiation rights. The EETPU claimed 716 members among the 1,500 workers at the factory. The TUC rebuked the EETPU but allowed its agreement to stand.[11] Hitachi reorganized work practices and made 508 workers redundant. The surrounding publicity focused not only on the 'war' between the EETPU and the other unions, but also on the acceptability or otherwise of 'no strike' deals (although they had not been an issue in the inter-union dispute). This media attention, the issues themselves, and the unrepentant stance of the EETPU resulted in the 1985 TUC Congress passing a resolution that expressed concern about unions entering agreements 'in circumstances which deprive other unions of their existing rights of recognition and negotiation'. In that year the EETPU signed a single-union deal at Yuasa Batteries, Ebbw Vale, and in 1987 another one at Orion Electric, Kenfig industrial estate, Port Talbot. In both cases the TGWU accused it of poaching members and the Orion case, together with one at Christian Salvesen (Food Services), resulted in the EETPU eventually being suspended from membership of the TUC on 8 July 1988 and subsequently expelled at the September congress after a combative speech by Eric Hammond its general secretary.[12]

It was a time of extreme bitterness within the WTUC and the TUC and valiant efforts were made by Norman Willis, in fear of a civil war breaking out within the union movement, to avoid the expulsion of the EETPU. The involvement of the EETPU in recruiting staff to work at Rupert Murdoch's print plant at Wapping infuriated the print unions and their allies, and the deals at Orion and Christian Salvesen in which TUC guidelines were broken were the last straw. Wyn Bevan, elected the EETPU's executive councillor for Wales and the south-west of England in 1979, was an ardent advocate of single-union 'no strike' deals. His uncompromising methods and success in signing such agreements with a majority of the Japanese firms in south Wales upset a number of unions, particularly the TGWU. It was widely believed that the EETPU was making too many concessions to these employers. Eight of the ten single-union deals signed with Japanese companies between 1985 and 1988 were with the EETPU.[13] At the 1987 WTUC conference George Wright created uproar by attacking Japanese companies that were employing 'samurai management' and wished to operate in 'a coolie economy' where they could have 'total subservience'.[14] The attack was all the more startling coming, as it did, from one so heavily involved in the promotion of inward investment. The following day the WTUC general council moved to dissociate the Wales TUC from the remarks but a rift between the TGWU and the electricians and the engineers remained. It was an issue that largely disappeared with the expulsion of the EETPU in 1988, the development by the TUC of revised guidelines and the growth of 'single-table bargaining' which co-ordinated the bargaining of different unions with the same employer. But not until the electricians merged with the engineers in 1992 to form the AEEU were they readmitted to the TUC (and WTUC) in 1993.

IN SEARCH OF A ROLE

Throughout the 1980s and up to 1997 the WTUC continued to express to the Welsh Office its concerns about unemployment, low pay, privatization, the need for skills training, health and safety and the protection and improvement of public services. Its arguments on the decline of manufacturing, the potential for growth among certain sectors and the importance of regional aid to manufacturers were substantiated by a series of reports commissioned from David Simpson of University College, Cardiff.[15] But the tide of opinion was against the trade unions. A third victory for Mrs Thatcher in 1987 brought a sober assessment of the strategy the Wales TUC should pursue. In a paper on campaigning in 1988, David Jenkins pointed out that there was

> Little merit in currently committing scarce resources to a campaign, for instance, against health service privatisation if it is that those currently receptive to the Wales TUC are already committed opponents of privatisation while those we seek to persuade and influence, the uncommitted middle ground of public opinion, are actually repelled, through ignorance or prejudice, by anything emanating from the trade union movement.

He therefore proposed that the campaign budget should be committed to improving the public's perception and awareness of the Wales TUC and the trade union movement in Wales.

Campaigns always took on a new urgency just before a general election and in the run-up to the 1992 election a series of documents concentrated upon low pay, health, the economy, Europe, training, housing, the rural economy and education. Yet once again Labour lost, this time to John Major, and later that year the industry minister Michael Heseltine announced that the remnants of the coal industry would have to be halved, with the loss of up to 30,000 jobs and the closure of thirty-one pits. Public opinion was outraged. The TUC organized a mass demonstration in London that attracted more than 200,000 people. The WTUC organized successful rallies throughout Wales, beginning at Cardiff City Hall, on the theme of 'Jobs and Recovery'. In March 1993 the government announced a partial and temporary reprieve for some of the pits. Inevitably the closures continued. But a new political mood was developing. The Tories were back in government yet there was a feeling that their time was running out.

Slowly the unions and the TUC had evolved a range of policies that seemed to offer a way forward. A defining moment came in September 1988 when Jacques Delors, President of the European Commission, addressed the TUC Congress. He brought a message that British trade unionists had been longing to hear. He emphasized the social dimension to the single market and spoke of social dialogue and collective bargaining as essential pillars of a democratic society. The developing Social Charter would emphasize workers' rights and endorse the role of trade unions as a social partner. The TUC had a major part to play in bringing the Social Charter to fruition.[16] He received a standing ovation; and the phrase was coined: 'Delors is our Shepherd'. Seven years earlier the TUC had voted for withdrawal from the European Union. Now Europe offered a vision that from the perspective of those standing in the wreckage of British trade unionism seemed extremely attractive. For historical reasons, labour relations in Europe had evolved a cooperative style of trade unionism. The contrast with Thatcherism could not have been greater, for here was a system that *by law* gave status to workers and their institutions. The emphasis was on partnership rather than upon the 'enemy within'. With Welshmen in several key positions within the European Commission and the Wales TUC's Co-operative Development Centre a beneficiary of European social funding the Wales TUC was already more focused on Europe than Congress House. The change of policy was welcomed.

John Monks took up the theme of partnership when he succeeded Norman Willis as general secretary of the TUC in 1993 and launched his 'new unionism' campaign in 1996. It was a two-pronged strategy. The first emphasized recruitment and organization and was uncontroversial. The second deliberately broke with the adversarial policies and practices of the past. Monks argued that unions should work with managements to maximize areas of agreement, deliver high standards of work, promote high levels of training in new skills and cooperate in increasing the added value of the enterprise. Messages that had been inherent in the WTUC approach to inward investment in the 1980s were now advanced on the national stage.

Another break with tradition came in the early 1990s when, in recognition of the weakness of their position and the inadequacies of collective bargaining, the unions abandoned their attachment to voluntarism and embraced the introduction of positive legal rights for all workers, unionists and non-unionists alike, because of their vulnerability in the labour market. At first advocating a statutory minimum wage and then going beyond it, the TUC began to campaign for equal rights for full- and part-time workers, a right to union recognition, restrictions on the length of working week, new rights to organize in the workplace and the right for all to have some kind of collective representation. It evolved as a package that in varying degrees the first Blair government conceded in the Employment Relations Act 1999.

In order to focus these campaigns Monks relaunched the TUC in 1994 by scrapping the standing committees of the general council, retaining only the women's and race committees, and placing more decision-making in the hands of an executive committee at the expense of the general council.[17] The Wales TUC, along with other TUC regional councils, followed a similar pattern in 1995 – and for similar reasons. The retention of the women's and race committees, and the subsequent emphasis put upon their work, was a deliberate attempt to widen the appeal of unions to groups under-represented in the movement. At the same time, the concept of social partnership was given priority in the field of productivity improvement through investment in skills. These priorities were particularly salient in Wales where new technologies had exposed the need to raise the skills of the labour force and where the growth of female employment pointed to the anomalous position of women within the trade union movement. Both issues had grown in acceptance throughout the life of the Wales TUC.

INVESTING IN PEOPLE

From its inception the Wales TUC grasped the importance of training to the Welsh economy. The paper prepared for the meeting with the Prime Minister Harold Wilson and his ministers on 10 October 1975 pointed out that Wales offered less training to young people entering employment than any other UK region and that the proportion of apprenticeships taken up in Wales was well below that in other development regions. It went on to argue that

> Greater attention should be given firstly, to the poor record of training opportunities offered by industry in Wales . . . and secondly on the need to plan and monitor future training facilities in Wales to meet the changing needs of an economy that is shifting away from primary and secondary industries – agriculture, extractive and manufacturing to tertiary industries – administration, services and distribution.[18]

This prescient statement was followed in January 1976 by a paper on the shortage of training opportunities for young persons in Wales, and in December 1977 by the publication of a ten-year strategy to resolve unemployment. This paid particular attention to the labour market (see p. 45). The rise in youth and adult unemployment in the 1980s meant that the Manpower Services Commission (MSC) became the main agency for managing the problems of unemployment. Representatives of the WTUC sat on the main Wales MSC board along with representatives of the CBI Wales. After the 1987 election the MSC was renamed the Training Commission and then in September 1988 the abolition of the

Commission was announced. It was replaced by Training and Enterprise Councils (TECs), locally based, employer-led, with much lower union representation and deliberately not constituted as representative bodies. In England some TECs dispensed with trade union involvement altogether (a different system operated in Scotland) but in Wales a trade union presence on each TEC was maintained.

By then the parlous state of training in Wales was a major cause of concern and from 1987 onwards the Wales TUC published annually a series of reports and papers advocating partnership between unions and employers to tackle the problem. The 1988 annual report emphasized the need for joint training committees within workplaces along the lines of joint health and safety committees. The 1991–2 annual report contained a comprehensive review of 'The Training Deficit – Wales' Wasted Talents'. It pointed out (in an echo of the 1975 paper) that the skills of the Welsh labour force were at a very low level compared with other areas of the UK and competing economies. The impressive training provision once supplied by the coal and steel industries had been largely lost. The growth of private services was producing low-skill, low-paid jobs. It concluded that skills development could not be left to 'the limited initiatives of Welsh employers'. The 1993–4 report highlighted findings from the Centre for Advanced Studies at University of Wales College of Cardiff, that the reliance upon inward investors should not be seen as a permanent phenomenon. The attraction of increasingly low-cost locations in eastern Europe, South America and south-east Asia would make it more difficult for Wales to attract investors. There was an urgent need to raise the level of skills in Welsh industry. Training was the key to future economic development.

Further reports reiterated the message and a substantial section of the 1995–6 annual report analysed the situation once again and announced a 'Bargaining for Skills' project whereby union representatives would promote and negotiate training for their members in the workplace. It was recognized, however, that this was far from a complete answer to the problem. In an analysis of the failures of the system David Jenkins pointed to the fact that employers alone decided what constituted an adequate level of training; that the system was entirely voluntary; that it encouraged the poaching of labour; and that employees had limited incentive to seek education and training, for pay and status were rarely linked to qualifications.

For progress to be made towards full employment the social partnership on training cannot be restricted to in-company, in-work training. It is essential that

the unemployed receive the same standard of training as those in employment,
with transferable skills and qualifications . . . a substantial development of our
education and training provision is required.[19]

The election of a Labour government in 1997 with a strong commitment
to training and lifetime learning gave a fresh impetus to training
provision. The devolution of education and training as a matter for the
Welsh Assembly Government (WAG) then transformed the role of the
Wales TUC in this area. A Wales Union Learning Fund, announced by
WAG in 1999, committed £250,000 for each of the next three years and,
by 2003, such was its success that the annual funding commitment had
grown to some £900,000. In addition the Wales TUC, with the support of
the Welsh Assembly Government, set up a Learning Services Unit to
offer support and training for trade unions in Wales on the whole range
of lifelong learning issues. Education and lifelong learning had become
a major activity of the Wales TUC.

A WOMAN'S PLACE

A trade unionism based upon the male manual worker found it hard to
come to terms with the increasing number of women in the workforce
and its many implications. The bitter dispute between women and their
union, the AUEW, at the Hoover factory, Merthyr, in the autumn of 1981
became notorious. A management demand for 160 compulsory
redundancies was met by the union with an insistence that women
should lose their jobs before men, although this cut across the company's
'first in, last out' policy. The company agreed to declare women canteen
workers redundant and then to transfer semi-skilled women from the
shopfloor to take over the canteen jobs. The women called in the Equal
Opportunities Commission, which advised the company that the
women could claim unfair dismissal. The Hoover management froze all
the redundancies and eventually integrated the women with the male
labour force throughout the factory, despite a flat refusal by the union
full-time officials to represent the women. If the AUEW had been
successful, it was claimed, then approximately one-third of the women
would have lost their jobs even though they comprised only a tenth of
the Hoover workforce.[20]

Cases like this in which women stood against specific unfair
treatment, the involvement of Welsh women in the Greenham Common

vigil, the women's support groups in the miners' strike of 1984–5 and the Blaenau Ffestiniog quarry workers' strike of 1985–6, and the declining proportion of male trade unionists brought home the principled and practical reasons why trade unions needed to address areas of concern that predominantly affect women such as equal pay, career progression and caring responsibilities. Women were more relevant to the unions than ever before. It was time for the unions to become relevant to women. Even so, it was a painful process for unions with predominantly male memberships to be told that they were out of date and conservative. Had they not always been in the vanguard of democracy and progress? The law, of course, through the Equal Pay Act 1970 and the Sex Discrimination Act 1975 together with the Race Relations Acts of 1968 and 1976, also underlined that the employment relationship was no longer the sole concern of white, male manual workers. In 1983 the WTUC general council agreed that crèche facilities should be provided at annual conferences, if notified in advance. In 1984 it set up a women's advisory committee. The issues were more complex, however, than just setting up a committee. There is no evidence that women are less willing than men to join a union but the gendered division of labour in households can create difficulties. Because of domestic responsibilities part-time work is frequently a necessary feature of many women's working lives and part-time workers are notoriously difficult to recruit into unions. Women's patterns of work also affect their union participation. A break following childbirth means that, whereas the typical male union member is in his forties and has years of work and union experience behind him, the typical female member may have only a few years experience. She consequently has less knowledge of union structure, practice and procedures. In an ageing society more and more women workers find themselves caring for elderly sick relatives, a role that often inhibits them from taking on the extra task of being a workplace representative.

These were difficulties that required recognition and then addressing. It took time to do so. Holding branch meetings in a workingmen's club ('no women allowed'), or without a crèche were the norm and deterred women from getting involved. Their development as branch officials and shop stewards was hindered by education courses arranged solely with male trade unionists in mind, who were able to attend evening classes or travel to courses. In one case the district official of the TGWU suggested that the female branch officers of a newly organized Ebbw Vale factory should give up a week of their summer holiday to attend a course. Not surprisingly this was rejected. But it perpetuated a situation in which the female branch officers and shop stewards were heavily dependent upon the full-time male district official in all their dealings with management.[21] Gradually other issues were recognized: the need for specific recruitment material aimed at part-timers; the need for more women full-time officers; assertiveness training in male-dominated industries; education about sexual harassment; equal pay for equal work; and child care generally.

The 1987 annual report reflected the greater priority given to making trade union membership attractive to women and set out the wide range of conferences and events held during the year with the purpose of 'demonstrating our willingness to work for women with a range of initiatives of practical benefit'. In 1988 the annual conference decided by a narrow majority to reserve three seats for women on the general council. NUPE, with a female membership of over 70 per cent, had set an example in the 1970s by reserving five places for women on its own executive council.[22] The 1989 and 1990 WTUC conferences passed resolutions calling for workplace nurseries and in 1991 came a further call for employers to provide care for employees' children under 5. Resolutions on domestic violence and women's health care followed. The 1998 report of the women's committee focused on the needs of carers in employment. Links were forged between the women's committee and Chwarae Teg, and the Equal Opportunities Commission in Wales. By the mid-1990s major sections of the WTUC annual report were dealing with equal opportunity issues.

These changes reflect the slow but steady increase in the involvement of women in the union movement in Wales and TUC priorities. By 1993 a high proportion of the students on Wales TUC education courses were women. There is a two-day women's conference. In 1998 both the chair and vice-chair of the WTUC were women. In the mid-1980s fewer than one in ten conference delegates were women and only two women sat on the general council in 1986–7. In 2003 29 per cent of conference delegates were female and twenty-one out of fifty-two members of the general council were female – 40 per cent; 35 per cent of the executive committee was female.

If strides have been made to bring women closer to the centre of policy-making, progress on race equality has been more hesitant. Attempts to set up a race relations advisory committee were made in the 1970s and 1980s but without consistent success.[23] But in May 1992 a conference on 'Racism – A Trade Union Issue', the first of its kind in Wales was jointly organized by the WTUC and South Glamorgan Race Equality Council.

The next year a race advisory committee was set up. In that year the death of the black teenager Stephen Lawrence in London led eventually to the Macpherson Report, published in 1999, which identified evidence of institutional racism within organizations. In response, the WTUC general council produced a strongly worded statement to the 2000 annual conference. The conference not only set up an elected WTUC race equality committee, but charged it with informing the general council on all matters to do with race discrimination, to raise awareness amongst unions in Wales, to organize an annual race equality conference and to report annually to the WTUC conference. In 2001 the first race equality conference was held in Cardiff City Hall, addressed amongst others by Paul Robeson Jnr – a reminder of the affinity that his father had with the trade union movement in Wales. In 2002 the WTUC annual conference agreed a rule change that reserved two seats on the general council for black and ethnic minority trade unionists. Today the race equality committee works actively with the Commission for Racial Equality in Wales to confront workplace racism and develop employment opportunities.[24] The equalities agenda is now one of the WTUC's three top priorities together with lifelong learning and promoting trade unionism through partnership.

TRANSPORT HOUSE V. CONGRESS HOUSE

A constant if underlying theme in the life of the Wales TUC has been a tension in its relationship with the British TUC. Born out of confrontation, rebellious over steel closures, going its own way over co-operative development, chafing at restraints imposed by the TUC and constantly feeling under-resourced, the Wales TUC has more than once threatened to go its own way. Occasionally the paymaster has played one tune and the Welsh dragon has danced to another. From its inception the Wales TUC had scarcely any resources of its own. Chapter 3 pointed out its reliance on the TGWU and on researchers funded by a grant from the Department of Trade and Industry. By 1978 it had acquired its first full-time employee (David Jenkins) and had flagged up the desire to appoint a full-time general secretary sometime in the early 1980s. This idea had been around from the earliest days of the WTUC but it was not seen as an urgent issue. There was no serious challenger to George Wright and there was a view that the organization needed time to establish itself before Wright handed over the reins. But as the political influence of the

TUC and the WTUC waned, both turned to an examination of their internal affairs.

In 1980 the TUC invited the WTUC to contribute to a major review of TUC operations. It was an opportunity too good to miss. The submission was wide-ranging and began by emphasizing the considerable increase in the work undertaken in recent years, the paucity of WTUC staff, and the greater resources available to the Labour Party and the CBI in Wales. In particular it drew attention to the range of functions and staffing of the Welsh Office.

> In funding and resourcing the Wales TUC it must be contended that the TUC have not fully evaluated the role of the Welsh Office in the structure of British Government nor the imminent changes which are about to occur in the prioritisation of much of government expenditure within Wales.

The submission went on to argue that the WTUC was seriously under-resourced.

> That the amateurism and superficiality of much of the Wales TUC's activities is not widely realised says much for the professionalism and ability of those who voluntarily give their time and effort to ensuring its success. It is increasingly doubtful, however, whether such a position within the economic and social life of Wales can be maintained without the injection of a considerably improved resource back-up service.[25]

The document pointed out that the WTUC's physical resources were two offices, rented from the TGWU, a telephone line, a typewriter, four filing cabinets and some shelving. It proposed two additional appointments – an assistant secretary (research) and an office shorthand typist – and reaffirmed that a full-time general secretary should be appointed early in the 1980s. There was also a plea that the TUC education officer in Wales should be integrated into the WTUC. The submission then proposed, in the cause of sound communication between the two bodies, that the WTUC should be represented at the annual TUC Congress, with speaking rights but not voting rights; that it should be represented without voting rights on the main TUC committees (but not the general council); and that the minutes of the WTUC general council should be placed before the TUC general council to be 'received' but not formally 'approved'.

It further argued that, in addition to its current functions, the Wales TUC should undertake three additional areas of responsibility. One would be to deal with local inter-union disputes through a Wales TUC disputes committee, a procedure followed in Scotland. Secondly, given that Wales was represented in the European Parliament, and that the EEC recognized Wales as a region and had an office in Cardiff, 'it is in practice impossible not to be drawn into arguments relating to Wales within the EEC'. The WTUC therefore sought closer liaison with the TUC on EEC regional matters and wanted to be included on delegations where aspects of policy relating to Wales were under discussion. Thirdly, the WTUC should be given responsibility for developing services for the growing number of unemployed people with funding for the task provided by the TUC.

These were bold demands and they have to be seen in the context of the disagreement that year between the TUC and the Wales TUC over the conduct of the steel strike and the protests in Wales against closures. The reference in the speech made by Wright at the 1980 conference to expecting 'a greater measure of self-determination', quoted above, reflected both frustration and a stage in the argument for greater autonomy. Most of the proposals were rejected but, as part of an initiative throughout the UK, the TUC funded a part-time organizer for unemployed centres in Wales: first Les Paul and later Hubert Morgan. By December 1981 over twenty centres in Wales were established or in the final stages of being set up and by the mid-1980s there were thirty.

The arguments surfaced again in 1985 when the Wales TUC conference passed a resolution put down by SOGAT82. This declared: 'Conference supports the objective of the Wales TUC establishing the same degree of autonomy as is afforded to the Scottish and Irish Trades Union Congresses. Conference calls on the General Council to initiate discussions with the TUC in this regard.' A variety of major problems confronting the TUC, including the issue of whether to accept government funding for the conduct of union ballots, delayed discussion before the 1986 WTUC conference. In the absence of any apparent progress the TGWU proposed a motion at the 1986 conference that reflected a position still nursed by Wright. It called for 'a completely autonomous and financially independent Wales TUC', and included the following sentence: 'Conference also instructs the General Council to prepare an alternative programme to achieve independence in the event of agreement not being reached with the TUC.'

During the debate Wright, on behalf of the TGWU, accepted an amendment put down by the National Communications Union. The amended and successful resolution deleted the sentence quoted above and the reference to a financially independent WTUC. All suggestion that the Wales TUC could become financially independent of the TUC and that autonomy could be achieved regardless of the TUC was thereby removed. But it did affirm support for an autonomous Wales TUC and instructed the general council to enter into discussions to achieve this objective. Not for the first time a trade union conference showed its ability to face both ways simultaneously. Subsequently the general council decided that discussion with the TUC should be around five broad principles. These were the right for the Wales TUC to determine its agenda; the right to administer its own organization; the right to deal with inter-union policy including disputes; the right to develop international relationships; and the right to develop improved servicing of the needs and requirements of trade unions in Wales.

Discussions took place with Norman Willis and other TUC officials and then finally with the TUC's finance and general purposes committee on 23 March 1987. At this meeting the WTUC representatives reiterated a number of the arguments made in 1980 and pointed out: 'the Wales TUC has never, since its inception, accepted a regional council status'. The response of the TUC general council was given in April. It pointed out that 'within TUC structures' it was recognized that the WTUC was different from the English regional councils in that it had a different constitution and more resources. However, the TUC did not 'believe there is a case for a change in relationships unless there are major changes in devolution of government functions in Wales, and to union structures within Wales'.[26] It recognized that there was a case for additional staff and resources to be allocated to the WTUC but, in a situation where the TUC's own income was reduced, an increase was not possible. However, it had no objection to additional funds being raised within Wales provided they were not used to employ extra staff. (Presumably the TUC was wary of being obliged to pay extra staff costs at some future date.) The general council also recognized the special status of Wales within the EEC and acceded to the WTUC the right to nominate a representative on appropriate EEC committees. The TUC response left the door open for helpful rule changes to take place. John Monks, then the head of the TUC organization department, approached the task positively. 'I started on the basis of what can we give them.'[27] The WTUC gained the right in rule to raise its own funds, provided that affiliated unions gave on a voluntary basis and that the money was spent on objects defined in a new rule. The WTUC had complete discretion over the interpretation of these objects, subject only to the Congress of the

TUC. The duties of the general council were revised so that the convening of a special conference no longer required the specific authority of the TUC – an issue that had rankled since 1980. These rule revisions were meant to put the autonomy issue to bed for the foreseeable future.

They did not. In 1991 the TUC, faced with increasing financial difficulties, proposed a cut of £8,000 in its grant to the Wales TUC, a reduction in real terms of 37 per cent. It drew a fierce response. The WTUC general council put a resolution to its annual conference that was carried unanimously. Once again the threat of greater autonomy was raised in paragraphs that read:

> Given the intention of Congress House to significantly reduce the level of TUC funding of the Wales TUC, Conference sees it as necessary to initiate a proper debate within the Movement as to both the funding and the resourcing of the Wales TUC and the future balance which should be struck between the TUC and direct union sources of funding.
>
> Conference calls on the General Council to initiate such discussions with member unions and to report their outcome to the 1992 Annual Conference.

In the event, discussions with John Monks and Brendan Barber secured a considerable concession from the TUC. But in 1992 the need for further economies at the TUC threatened the post of research and administrative officer in Wales. With the WTUC operating on a total staff complement of three, the loss of one post was seen as potentially calamitous. Another round of discussions ensued and once again the TUC conceded but found a way of making economies in an area then outside the remit of the Wales TUC. The TUC education officer for Wales now became responsible in addition for the south-west of England, a situation that continued until April 2003.

The relaunch of the TUC in 1994 was followed in 1996 by a review of the purposes and functions of the TUC's regional machinery. The conclusions of the review reflected the new TUC emphasis on campaigning and delivering key services. The regional councils and trades councils were seen as 'delivery routes' for agreed national priorities. An annual work programme reflecting these priorities, as well as region-specific issues, was now agreed with the TUC. And in 2000 the TUC's education service and staff were fully integrated with the regional council structure.[28] It was clearly an attempt by the TUC to take a firmer grip upon the activities of its regional arms. But for the Wales TUC, in a country on the brink of democratic devolution, new and different pressures were about to arise.

Chapter 6

Devolution and After

A new political culture is emerging in the UK, offering new opportunities for the TUC and unions to get the voice of working people heard. (Brendan Barber)

In one generation the world inhabited by the Wales TUC has changed irrevocably. In 1974 trade unions were at the height of their post-war influence. Senior members of the TUC general council were constant visitors to Downing Street. Six out of ten Welsh workers were in a trade union. Car workers and miners were the militant spearhead of the working class, embodying a tradition of struggle stretching back to Dic Penderyn. No one had heard of the internet, mobile phones or call centres. An elected Welsh Assembly, high on the WTUC's priorities, was a quarter of a century in the future. Now, early in the twenty-first century, trade unions in Wales and their representative body, the Wales TUC, face urgent questions concerning power and influence, the relevance of tradition, the role of ideology and whether they have the capacity for renewal. These are themes of this chapter.

THE STANDARD BEARER

At first sight the Wales TUC has come full circle. Its early years with Labour in power and John Morris as Secretary of State provided it with access to the highest levels of government. Next came almost eighteen years of Tory rule when it was pushed to the margins of policy-making and, although consistently expressing the voice of trade unionism in Wales, it was largely impotent outside the area of economic development. Today, with a Labour majority in the Welsh Assembly Government (WAG) and at Westminster, it once again has access to Cabinet Ministers and the opportunity to influence policy across the board. But appearances can be deceptive. From its earliest days the Wales TUC was a standard bearer for devolutionary politics. Now that it is here, devolution provides an opportunity yet to be grasped by most trade unions, and it comes when trade unions and the Wales TUC are at their weakest, following years of membership loss and decline in authority.

The 1974 Wales TUC inaugural conference called for 'the early setting up of an elected Legislative Assembly for Wales' with powers to deal with the many industrial, economic and social problems in Wales. This ensured 'that Welsh politics also embraced the Welsh economy and consequently made the devolution argument more broadly based'.[1] It also made certain in those early years that devolution remained high on Labour's agenda. As the *Western Mail* noted on 26 April 1976:

> Without the creation of the Wales TUC three years ago it is doubtful whether the government's Welsh Assembly proposals would have got off the ground. And without the Wales TUC's persistent and unfaltering pressure, it is doubtful whether the Assembly would reach fruition.[2]

Part of that persistent pressure was a trenchant document arguing for an elected assembly with powers very similar to those that now exist. Trade union votes at Labour Party conferences in the 1970s ensured that the proposals on devolution for Wales were endorsed. The WTUC also rejected the use of a referendum to determine the matter.[3] But when the Labour government chose that route George Wright and other union officials took a leading part in the devolution campaign of 1978–9 – 'a shambles' in Wright's opinion, 'the Labour Party staff went on holiday'. And although the issue was submerged by the defeat of 1979 it resurfaced from time to time in the Wales TUC and increasingly among Labour Party supporters as a reaction to the domination of Wales by a Tory government. By 1992 the national Labour Party rather unenthusiastically had reached the point of including in its election manifesto a commitment to devolution. When that election ended in yet another defeat, the Wales TUC reflected the frustration felt in Wales by passing an emergency resolution at its annual conference calling for a Welsh Constitutional Convention along Scottish lines; and a document was prepared out of which such a convention might emerge. The Wales Labour Party executive, suspicious of cross-party organizations, rejected this and set up a Constitutional Policy Commission. From that point the road led, with many a twist and turn, to the successful referendum result in 1997.[4] Trade unions played an important part in funding the Yes campaign of 1997 with Unison, for example, providing £10,000 and the

Wales TUC being represented on the Yes for Wales Campaign Committee. In June 1997 the WTUC published *Making Our Voice Heard*, a supporting document that was widely circulated.

THE CHALLENGE OF DEVOLUTION

The Government of Wales Act 1998 puts trade unions in Wales and the Wales TUC into a situation completely different from any previously known. The Welsh Assembly Government now has a duty to consult with the business sector and that includes trade unions and the Wales TUC. This is not merely a huge reversal of the marginalization that took place between 1979 and 1997; it places upon a formal footing the open-door policy that prevailed when John Morris was Secretary of State. But the WTUC is not in a privileged position. There is a statutory requirement that the government in Wales consults, through partnership councils, with local government and the voluntary sector. Only in Wales is such consultation subject to a statutory requirement. Neither in Scotland nor in London do such provisions exist. Furthermore this government, more open than any other in Wales in the past, has wider responsibilities than those formerly held by the Welsh Office. These include industrial, economic and social development, education and training, the health service in Wales, agriculture, forestry, fisheries and food, local government, housing, social services, transport, planning and the environment, arts, culture and the Welsh language. On all these matters the WAG issues a flood of consultative documents.

The consultative process is crucial. As the Assembly is a single-chamber form of government, influence must be exerted long before an issue reaches the floor of the chamber. In addition to written responses to some twenty consultative documents in a year, the Wales TUC makes its views known through meetings with ministers and senior civil servants. There is a minimum of two formal meetings each year with the First Minister accompanied by Cabinet members – but usually there are double that number of such meetings. There are frequent meetings ('more than ten but less than twenty') with ministers, particularly those heading the departments of greatest concern to the WTUC – economic development, education, social justice and health. Two formal arrangements provide the framework for these meetings. The Business Partnership Council that comprises business organizations, trade unions and 'not for profit' companies meets in formal session three times a year. It is chaired by the First Minister, and discusses strategic issues and any deficiencies in the consultation process. Its meetings are held in public and the council is the visible manifestation of the consultative process that continues day by day. Initially the Wales TUC had one seat on the council and business interests had 'at least five'. Now the same formula applies to the WTUC and representation is roughly equal.

The second arrangement is more important to the Wales TUC. Although happy to work with employers through the Business Partnership Council on issues of industrial and economic development, the Wales TUC has a much broader agenda encompassing the social dimensions of government policy. Consequently, discussions with WAG led to the signing at Transport House, Cardiff, on 5 February 2003 of a Memorandum of Understanding between the Welsh Assembly Government and the Wales TUC. The aim of the memorandum 'is to establish effective co-operation between the Welsh Assembly Government and the Wales TUC'. Both parties agreed to focus on five priorities: economic development in Wales, improved levels of education and training, public service modernization, promotion of equal opportunities and social partnership. These initial priorities may be amended at future meetings. The memorandum also provides for a joint secretariat, drawn from the Wales TUC and policy advisers to the WAG, which will monitor all matters relating to the memorandum and promote its effective operation. The intention, says David Jenkins, is for 'hearts and minds to move together'. Although the Scottish Parliament and the Scottish TUC have signed a similar document, this memorandum is unique in Wales.

One other piece of machinery should be mentioned. In the early days of the WAG the Wales TUC found itself overwhelmed by the number of documents on which it was expected to comment. In response to this outbreak of 'consultationitis' – and which similarly affected employers' organizations – a social partners' unit was formed, funded by the WAG and jointly managed by the WTUC and Business Wales (a consortium of employers organizations, including CBI Wales and the Wales Chamber of Commerce). It acts as the eyes and ears of the business and trade union sector, identifying key issues not only in the Assembly but also in Westminster and the European Union.

Finally, on non-devolved matters such as employment law or Treasury decisions, there are meetings between the WTUC executive and the Secretary of State for Wales accompanied by Welsh Office ministers. Again, such formal meetings are supplemented by informal occasions. For these discussions the Wales TUC draws upon the research resources of the TUC.

That the WTUC is recognized as a social partner in the development of Wales does not automatically mean that its influence will grow or even be sustained. It is in a highly competitive situation. The requirement upon the WAG to consult with a wide range of bodies means that there are many well-resourced organizations putting forward different views from those of the trade unions. The extent to which the Wales TUC is able to influence decisions depends upon the quality of its presentations and the issues it chooses to pursue. These in turn largely depend upon the strength and will of the unions that affiliate to it and the extent to which they agree a policy and follow it through. In this new situation the question arises: can the trade union movement in Wales, representing nearly half a million workers, ensure that their views have an impact upon the decisions of the WAG? As one experienced participant commented: 'Under the Tories the job of the WTUC was easier. There was an excuse for no progress. That no longer applies.'

FACING THE CHALLENGE

For the first twenty-five years of its history the WTUC emphasized its distinctiveness; so much so that even TUC general secretaries were lulled at times into referring to it as a separate entity. It had a consistent message. Wales is not a region but a country. Wales is different from England in language, values, trade union consciousness; in having a variety of devolved economic, social and artistic institutions. There is a Welsh Office and a Secretary of State for Wales in the Cabinet. In its first year the Wales TUC designed its own logo. All this was in order to argue for more freedom and more resources. In truth, for most of its life, a general secretary, a researcher/administrator and an office secretary have been its only staff.

Once the result of the 1997 referendum became known, it was evident that more resources would be required to cope with Assembly business. On 14 December 1998 representatives of the WTUC met John Monks, general secretary of the TUC, to discuss the resources and functioning of the Wales TUC in the light of the decision to establish a National Assembly for Wales. The WTUC briefing paper set out the case for enhanced funding to meet the challenge of devolution. It pointed out that:

> The trade union movement will need to ensure that a trade union input is
> made into the deliberations of the Assembly Subject Committees and the policy

formulations of the Executive committee . . . For many trade unions, particularly for those with membership working in areas such as education, health or transport which are directly affected by the transfer of devolved powers to the Assembly, this will require their own specific consideration of resources and any organisational response. For all unions, it requires consideration by the TUC both in terms of an equitable distribution of resources and how best to respond to the organisational and structure effects of devolution . . . To date the TUC has not fully recognised the implications for the Movement of devolved government structures.[5]

Further meetings with the TUC resulted in it funding an assistant general secretary in addition to the general secretary, the research officer and an administrative assistant. But, as indicated in Chapter 5, the TUC in 2000 integrated its trade union education staff into the Wales TUC structure, a long overdue move, finally prompted by the devolution of educational affairs to the Assembly. By this means three extra staff were acquired. Their work remains primarily the education of trade union activists but there is some flexibility of tasks within the office.

A separate and highly significant development has been the growth of the learning services unit within the WTUC. Developing from a concern to improve workplace skills and communications the unit now promotes all areas of lifelong learning. Hard lobbying on the importance of lifelong learning and the contribution that the WTUC could make to its dissemination, resulted in April 2003 in a contract with the Assembly that provided £1.4 million over three years to fund the equivalent of ten full-time posts. These include five locally based development officers and two support workers who cover the whole of Wales. The Wales TUC has added the development of lifelong learning to its traditional roles of lobbying and campaigning.

There has also been a shift of focus in its campaigning. The development of labour law now provides individuals with protection against abuse of power and promotes equality of treatment. Consequently, WTUC campaigns on equality and anti-discrimination are aimed at employers and employees rather than at the government. The unions are now upholders of individual employment law in the workplace, just as they have been for health and safety during the past thirty years. The growth of the non-discrimination principle and its application to gender, racial or ethnic origin, religion or belief, disability, age and sexual orientation ensures a continuing role for the WTUC in these matters. The WTUC has come in from the cold and, in another well-worn cliché, is seen now as a source of solutions rather than the cause of problems. The

Memorandum of Understanding signifies its recognition as a social partner in the development of Wales. The additional funding from the TUC and the Assembly is provided for the WTUC to carry out its priority tasks: contributing to economic development in Wales through the learning and skills agenda; promoting equal opportunities and campaigning against discrimination; and developing partnerships with the Assembly and in the workplace.

The work of the learning services unit is an interesting example of the new approach. Low skills are a serious problem in Wales. Twenty per cent of the Welsh population of working age have no formal qualifications. Only in Northern Ireland is the situation worse. The Wales TUC document *Economic Development and Regeneration* claims that one in four of the Welsh population is functionally illiterate and two in five functionally non-numerate.[6] The result is that many organizations in the public and private sectors are, without realizing it, employing people with inadequate basic skills and workers have limited job horizons. It is not only an economic issue but an equality one too, because inadequate skills stunt aspirations and prevent the full achievement of individual potential.

The learning services unit works closely with unions to bring learning opportunities into the workplace. Its development officers help unions to negotiate learning agreements with managements, recruit workplace learning representatives, and enable learners to access funds from the Individual Learning Accounts scheme and unions to draw funds for learning from the Wales Union Learning Fund – worth over £900,000 in 2004. The content of courses varies but it is by no means restricted to technical skills. A high percentage of courses focuses on reading, writing, computer skills and Welsh language, but workers have requested sign language, art and design, and psychology among other examples. The teachers are usually staff from further education colleges or the Workers' Educational Association. Key figures in these developments are the unpaid union learning representatives in the workplace. They have the legal right to 'reasonable' paid time off from work to carry out their duties. These include identifying the skills that fellow workers would like to acquire, providing information about learning and negotiating with employers and learning providers to arrange that learning. Already thousands of employees are benefiting every year from this programme and the ambitious target is to reach two-thirds of organized workplaces by 2006. In November 2003 the Wales TUC, together with CBI Wales, the National Council for Education and Learning in Wales and the Assembly government, signed a skills concordat in which all four organizations undertook to work together to raise the skills of working people.

The WTUC can point to successes too in its traditional role of lobbying government. Perhaps the most significant has been to persuade the Assembly government and its executive agencies to adopt workplace partnership as a key strategy for economic development; a declaration also endorsed by CBI Wales and the Engineering Employers Federation. Subsequently a partnership agreement was signed in 2003 between the National Assembly and the trade unions representing Assembly staff in which they both commit to work together on matters of common interest. Another successful area has been the campaign to increase investment in publicly owned services and to safeguard the terms and conditions of employees transferred from the public sector into the private. So far as relations with the Welsh Assembly Government are concerned, the Memorandum of Understanding, the Skills Concordat, the Declaration on Workplace Partnerships and a joint campaign with the Assembly and the Equal Opportunities Commission on equal pay all point to a fruitful relationship. Relations with the Westminster government are less so. On issues of employment law and help for the manufacturing sector, the TUC finds the government wanting. But access by the WTUC to the Secretary of State for Wales enables the case for Welsh manufacturing to be regularly presented. With the programme of the Labour government in Wales the product of conferences and discussions in which trades unions have played a major part, it should not be surprising that a high degree of policy convergence exists between the WTUC and the Welsh Assembly Government. This, however, is not the whole story.

THE VIEW FROM THE BAY

Experienced and knowledgeable insiders have a range of criticisms of the impact that the Wales TUC and individual trade unions make upon Assembly decision-makers. The fundamental one is that the trade union voice is not heard loudly enough. A Labour Assembly Member remarked on this and added:

> The voluntary sector and the agricultural lobby are very evident; they always have a place at the table. The voluntary sector is way ahead at getting its voice heard and at setting the agenda. Their voice is reflected in every policy paper. When the trade union voice is heard it is invariably defensive; complaining

about ASW pensions or Friction Dynamics. Which is fine as far as it goes but they are not coming up with positive policy ideas. Trade unions are just reactive and lack ideas. They need to catch up with the fact that devolution has taken place. The door is wide open for them.

A lobbyist made exactly the same points and claimed: 'a huge amount of business is done without a union input. Assembly officials simply do not think "trade union" and papers are prepared without any mention of unions whatsoever.' This may be true in some departments, but not in all. The WTUC's long history of lobbying the Welsh Office on industrial matters ensures that civil servants dealing with the economy *are* conscious that unions have a role. There is general agreement that the teaching unions have adapted quickly to the demands of devolution and that the Education and Lifelong Learning department is well aware of the interests of the unions.

But a more fundamental criticism was raised in relation to union delegations generally. A senior employee of the Assembly said:

> They turn up and just chat. The pre-work hasn't been done. It's amateur. They depend on contacts made in the past, the fact that we all know each other; it's labour movement cosiness. They have this belief that if things go seriously wrong they can pick up the phone to Rhodri. The representations from the employers are much better.

A trade union leader made a similar point. 'There was frustration among unions affiliated to the Labour Party during the period of coalition government. They wanted more access to ministers and felt they should be able to pick up the phone to Rhodri.' Interestingly, some confirmation of these points comes from David Jenkins:

> When Labour came in the Wales TUC actually lost influence because each individual union had access to the Assembly. The unions affiliated to the Labour Party were picking the phone up to the Assembly Members they had sponsored. It is not the way to have long-term influence. The WTUC influence is on the rise again now after a dip when unions tried to do things on their own.[7]

At times, it has been a hard struggle to get heard. 'The civil service instinct is *not* to think trade union. Most of them were recruited and trained under Thatcher.'

In some eyes inadequate resources remain a problem for a Welsh trade union movement confronted by a greater range and weight of consultation than ever before. It is pointed out that union head office staffs have not grasped the implications of devolution – the fact that Wales is pursuing different policies from England in certain areas – and nor have their regional officers thought hard enough about the difference. The TGWU, which has operated as an all-Wales region since the late 1960s, is the only one of the major unions that has a researcher in Wales. There is a view that other major unions believe that Wales is so small that even they cannot justify research dedicated solely to Welsh problems. If that is so then the research and representative task is back in the hands of the secretary and assistant secretary and the one researcher of the Wales TUC: resources already seen by some as being spread too thinly. A robust contrary view was expressed in the following terms.

> The unions and the WTUC deal too much in generalisations, They should bring specific examples of how policies are not working rather than just expressing opposition. This requires unions to give the WTUC concrete examples, or for the WTUC to ask for them. If unions lobby hard, lobby the right person, and present concrete facts instead of generalisations, they can change minds. If they concentrated on devolved matters the WTUC would have enough resources.

Clearly the issues raised by these comments are matters for the Wales TUC and its affiliated unions to consider and judge. But devolution in Scotland, Northern Ireland and London, and the moves towards elected regional assemblies in England, are presenting precisely the same challenges to the unions in those localities. How can they exert influence upon decision-takers in the face of arguments from organizations that have equal access and are better resourced? How can the research and other resources available to unions in the regions be increased? In this new and evolving situation are the TUC and individual unions too centralized?

Some ideas have already emerged. The Scottish TUC e-mailed all the Scottish higher education and research institutions to ask if people would be interested in participating in a Scottish trade union research network. It now has a network of industrial relations specialists, economists and political scientists, plus engineers, biochemists, architects and accountants.[8] Similar developments have taken place in London and in the TUC's north-eastern region. The shortage of suitable individuals to represent the trade union view on a wide range of local and regional

bodies has been recognized by the north-eastern region, as has the critical
need for officers and activists to receive education and training on issues
related to governance, policy-making and civil society. In partnership
with the Centre for Urban and Regional Development Studies at Newcastle
University, a course has been developed to provide knowledge and
understanding of what is required.[9]

PARTNERSHIP OR INCORPORATION?

The concept of partnership, embraced with enthusiasm by the Wales
TUC, is a controversial one. It raises fundamental questions about the
role of trade unions in the workplace and at the level of the state. The
involvement of British trade union leaders – generally through the TUC
– with the machinery of the state goes back to at least the First World
War. But with the post-1945 Keynesian consensus and lengthy periods of
Labour rule the unions became involved in incomes policies, partici-
pated in tri-partite planning machinery and, in the 1970s, in the detailed
drafting of legislation. These developments were viewed with suspicion,
depending upon the viewpoint, as being either a device to smother the
power of organized labour, or an unwelcome enhancement of trade
union power in relation to the state. The breakdown of the Social
Contract followed by the 'Winter of Discontent' and then Mrs Thatcher's
administration, ended all such discussion. The Blair governments, wary
of the history, have kept the unions at arm's length. But the Welsh
Assembly Government has accepted the Wales TUC as a social partner.
Wales is different.

For the best part of a century there has been a rejection in Wales of the
concept of a laissez-faire political economy. Instead there has developed
an alternative vision and an alternative set of values. There is still in
Wales a belief in social democracy, that government action can produce
a better social order and that trade unionism has a legitimate place in
society. When this labourism is combined with a large public sector and
a sense of Welsh identity that looks to 'the national interest', it is not
surprising that a corporate bias exists. It enabled the Wales TUC to form
a social partnership with the Tories on the restricted area of inward investment. It would be extraordinary if the Wales TUC did not work with
the Assembly for economic development and equality. Unlike past
corporatist examples, the unions have not been asked to restrain their
collective-bargaining demands. So long as the WTUC remains free to

campaign and lobby on behalf of workers and their families, and is not inhibited from doing so, there should be no clash of interests.

WORKPLACE PARTNERSHIP

Controversy also surrounds the issue of partnership in the workplace, for it marks a clear break with a strong tradition of militancy in Welsh trade union history. The trade union movement is by origin and definition one of protest against the unequal and exploitative employment relationship. It is management's job to direct workers' labour power in ways that produce a surplus for the enterprise. Because of this the relation between management and worker, between capital and labour, has been called one of 'structured antagonism'.[10] Workers and employers do have different interests. Yet day-to-day cooperation is essential, for the surplus that is produced is in the interests of the workers as well as the employers. Without the surplus, wages cannot be paid and the enterprise may collapse.

Is partnership between capital and labour possible when labour is being exploited to produce a surplus? In 1912 Welsh miners produced a historic pamphlet arguing for reform of their union, the South Wales Miners' Federation. They set out their ideas in uncompromising language:

> A united industrial organization, which, recognizing the war of interest between workers and employers, is constructed on fighting lines, allowing for a rapid and simultaneous stoppage of wheels throughout the mining industry . . . The old policy of identity of interest between employers and ourselves be abolished and a policy of open hostility installed.[11]

The promulgation of this theory of class war, combined with the appalling ignorance and vindictiveness of quarry and coal owners between 1890 and 1939 – who seemed determined to illustrate the validity of the theory – gave Welsh labour a reputation for militancy in the face of oppression. The milestones that mark modern Welsh trade union history tell of prolonged battles that usually ended in defeat: the miners' strike of 1898, the Penrhyn lock-out of 1900–3, the Cambrian Strike of 1910–11, the lock-out of 1926, the miners' strike of 1984–5. The courage and dedication of those who stood against injustice has made each defeat a badge of honour and the drama of these conflicts, illuminating relationships in whole communities, has been seized upon by historians and made the dominant theme of Welsh labour history.

But these events are only part of the story. The antagonism built into the relationship between management and worker does not inevitably lead to war. Different social relations are created by different kinds of industries and different patterns of work. Away from the geological conditions, declining productivity, and collapse of an export-based product market that made the South Wales Coalfield a battlefield, the history of trade unionism in Wales is very different. In the coalfield of north-east Wales it is a polar opposite.[12] In the steel and tinplate industries the conciliation boards that ensured many years of increased earnings and industrial peace in Wales are hardly ever mentioned. The steady growth of trade unionism in a multiplicity of industries and services, the development of collective bargaining and of joint industrial councils are neglected topics in Welsh trade union history. It is, after all, difficult to make high drama out of the minutes of a joint industrial council. A minute of the Joint Wages Board of Local Authorities of Glamorgan held on 26 September 1929 is not untypical: 'After hearing Mr Hopkins and Councillor Frank Quick it was agreed to recommend the local authorities to supply full-time lavatory attendants with a complete uniform and part-time lavatory attendants with a cap only.' Yet this illustrates the major day-by-day preoccupation of trade unionism: the conditions of work of labour.

Of course, collective bargaining over pay and conditions is not the same as partnership. On the contrary it focuses on an area where workers and employers have different interests – the distribution of the surplus. That remains a fundamental trade union task. Partnership implies going a stage further. It means working with management *to find ways to increase the surplus*. That in turn requires two conditions: an employer willing to enter into genuine partnership; and trade unions strong enough to be taken seriously as partners. The problem in Wales, as elsewhere, is not one of ideology but of practicality. After the Thatcher/Major years, employers no longer take collective bargaining for granted. Many employers see trade unions as disruptive of relations with their employees. In many parts of the private sector trade unionism is almost non-existent. The proportion of the working population in unions now is no higher than sixty years ago when Britain emerged from the 1930s depression into war. In many parts of the private sector the conditions for collective bargaining, let alone partnership, are absent.

There are some trade unionists that take comfort from the fact that trade union density in Wales is the highest in Great Britain. There are two problems with that. First, most trade unionists are in the public sector and the high level of trade union density in that sector distorts the overall picture. Union density in the public sector in Wales is 69 per cent. In the private sector it is 24 per cent.[13] The second problem is that the origins of the trade union culture that exists in Wales can be traced to an eruption of trade unionism between 1898 and 1920. It had an enormous influence that has finally run its course. On the railways, in the docks and quarries, in coal, steel and tinplate, among teachers, local authority workers and post office employees, the virtues of and necessity for trade union membership increasingly became a matter of faith in those early years. And the concentration of occupations in a few major industries enabled trade unionism to develop strong foundations. In 1921 miners and quarrymen, transport and metal workers made up 43 per cent of the employed population.[14] A tradition of collective organization was then handed down to the next generation and subsequently transferred by displaced miners and steelworkers into the new factories and workplaces after 1945. High levels of employment then helped to build the workplace trade unionism of the 1960s and 1970s. It was this tradition of strong trade unionism that the Wales TUC emphasized to inward investors. It was 'part of the Welsh way of doing things' and the success of that campaign in the 1970s and 1980s is another reason why trade union density in Wales is comparatively high. But the tradition is dying. Old age and death, having gripped the men who carried the trade union traditions of coal and steel, are now busily at work among the men and women who worked in the post-war factories. The return of mass unemployment after 1979, particularly the high levels of unemployment among the young, broke the chain. Employees aged above 40 have the highest union density at around 40 per cent. Only 20 per cent of those aged 20 to 29 are union members. The figure for those under 20 falls to less than 10 per cent. Before there can be significant partnerships in the private sector there will have to be a resurgence of trade unionism. This is the dilemma. The TUC believes that partnership is a means to renewal for trade unions but without renewal there cannot be genuine partnership.

How can the dilemma be resolved? Various observers have pointed out that a campaigning and organizing trade unionism does not sit easily with attempts to develop social partnerships with the government and with employers' associations.[15] Yet research studies 'clearly show that neither government legislation nor managerial support will act as substitutes for trade union organizing and campaigning'.[16] In the aftermath of the Thatcher/Major years, and with the return of high levels of employment, the trade unions need a coherent narrative that explains their modern purpose. It has to begin, like partnership, in the workplace. Surveys consistently show that the areas of work that are important to workers are: the quality of the working experience; prospects for promotion and self-improvement; having a voice in working arrangements; job security; and gender equality. They show that job satisfaction is less today than ten years ago, particularly for skilled manual male workers and semi and unskilled women workers. We also know that more than half of all employees in Wales are women and that the labour force as a whole is ageing, with an increasing proportion over 50.[17]

The narrative has to begin with these issues. There is now a consensus that unions should widen their collective-bargaining agenda and make clear to employees and employers that they have a positive contribution to make to individual welfare and to enterprise efficiency. The lead area is lifelong learning where employees, unions and employers cooperate to mutual benefit. Clare Jenkins, head of the WTUC lifelong learning unit, says

> There is close working between unions and WTUC on workplace learning. Unions see the work as important for recruitment and retention. It is a tangible thing; and it brings good publicity. Employers see the point. It is not a contentious area, it helps to raise productivity and benefits individuals. For the unions it's positive and helps to get partnership deals.

Partnership agreements on lifelong learning can be seen as helping to increase the surplus. Can the unions extend that concept to health and safety, equal pay, flexible working hours, pensions, bullying and discrimination? And do that in the new small workplaces where there are few union members? The issues chime with the concerns of employees as expressed in surveys, and contribute to improving workplace efficiency. They seem the most likely basis for a recruitment campaign. Unquestionably, the task is a daunting one. It would be interesting to see the result of a co-ordinated campaign by private sector unions, working with the Wales TUC, which concentrated efforts on a particular geographical area of Wales where service industry is growing.

The loss of bargaining strength inside the workplace since the heady days of the 1970s is a reminder that trade unions have traditionally had a broader agenda and a wider purpose. In the often quoted words of Allan Flanders, trade unions have 'two faces, sword of justice and vested interest'.[18] The Wales TUC has always campaigned on the wider social and economic issues. Campaigning is a reminder that union members are also consumers and citizens, and that trade unions cannot be just service agencies, learning organizations and processors of conference motions. But at a time when they seek to recover from years of decline, campaigning is also a means by which unions can forge alliances with community groups and expand their political influence. In the 1970s and 1980s the big issues were poverty, low wages, low skills and jobs worth having, all in the context of high and rising unemployment. The same problems remain but in a time of economic growth. Since the post-war Attlee government there has been a struggle in Wales to improve economic and social conditions and erase inequalities.

One example of where the Wales TUC could campaign on a variety of issues is the deindustrialization of the 1980s and 1990s that made the Valleys of south Wales one of the poorest areas of the European Union. The recent Bevan Foundation report on the Valleys drew attention once again to problems of inequality, inadequate transport, unemployment, environmental degradation, poor health, low pay and low skills. The Welsh Assembly Government's own *The Wales Spatial Plan* notes that the Valleys are characterized by very low rates of economic activity, a fact the Wales TUC first argued in 1989 and re-emphasized in 1993 as being a major cause of poverty.[19] *The Spatial Plan* further notes that, in the mid and upper Valleys: 'The skill base is poorly matched by the job opportunities arising there or within the coastal belt and there remain significant and persistent concentrations of multiple deprivation.' The problems are so deep-seated that Objective One funding from the European Union will not be sufficient to remove them. There may be difficulties for the Wales TUC in campaigning on behalf of one particular area (although the rural economy has been a subject of its support in the past) but the nature of the problems, the proportion of the Welsh population affected, and the emotional resonance of 'the Valleys problem' – well understood by Peter Walker when he was Secretary of State – would justify the Wales TUC making this a priority. Such a campaign would raise its profile and find allies in local authorities, voluntary organizations and the MPs and Assembly Members who represent the valley constituencies. And these are communities that have a strong sense of Welsh identity and where a campaigning trade unionism would be welcomed.

REFLECTIONS

Thirty years is a very short time in the life of an organization. But it has been the fate of the Wales TUC first to pass through a watershed for the trade union movement, and then another for the governance of Wales. To take the second first. Those thirty years have seen a massive increase in the powers and resources of the Welsh Office and then the National Assembly. Beyond those new powers an elected Assembly brings a new dimension to Welsh political life and decision-making. It creates Assembly Members who have their own constituency interests to look after. Against that it brings majority rule and party discipline. In its consultative arrangements it is more wide-ranging and more open than any previous Welsh administration. And as government responsibilities have expanded, bringing with them increasing numbers of civil servants, there has grown an emphasis upon administrative detail and problem-solving. 'Don't bring me problems, bring me solutions' is the cry of every decision-maker. Finally, the Assembly, through the devolved areas of public service, is the largest employer in Wales. It also subvents private industry and services to the tune of many millions of pounds. It has the power to promote partnership and consultation in those areas.

For the Wales TUC most of the past decade has been a time of working hard to stand still. Along with the TUC and the trade unions as a whole, its prestige and authority have declined. The reasons for this are well rehearsed: the Winter of Discontent and the following backlash, the political marginalization by Tory governments, the considerable loss of membership and representative credibility, the decline of national bargaining. There has also been a withering of the grass roots, particularly amongst the trades councils. But they have also been years of development. The early years of turmoil and protest established it as a political force in Wales with entry to Downing Street. It displayed a capacity for innovation that more than once caused Len Murray to say in envy, 'I wish we [the TUC] did not have a hundred years of history.' It rode the storm after 1979, participating in a way unique in Britain in economic development and trade union recruitment. And it celebrates those thirty years with more resources than ever before and as a recognized social partner in the building of a new Wales. In December 2003 David Jenkins announced that, after twenty years as general secretary, he would stand down at the thirtieth anniversary conference in 2004. He reflected that: 'Despite the Dark Ages for trade unionism from 1979 to 1997 we kept the flag flying in Wales and we've established workplace and social partnerships ahead of developments in the rest of the UK.' He remains confident that the trade unions have a bright future in Wales and that they should 'seize the chance that devolution now offers'.[20]

Nonetheless the task of rebuilding the unions remains difficult. The issue of partnership is contentious and there will be a price to be paid if unions are not strong. Where employers are not cooperative partnership is not the answer.

> If partnership is indeed to provide unions with a means of renewal, or survival, they will have to pursue agreements in the service sector, the key growth area in the economy . . . Not all unions will want to pursue agreements in the service sector if they are seen to limit union rights . . . they will need to build union membership and strong workplace structures in those service sector companies where employers show a propensity for partnership. They will need to demonstrate their worth both to prospective members and to their employers.[21]

A new and important development will follow the acceptance by the British government of the EU Directive on Information and Consultation Rights. This will open up channels of communication between management and employees that will *not* be union-based but which, in the current climate, unions should support and try to build on. It is one of the strengths of the Wales TUC that its aspirations towards equality and social justice are in line with the social philosophy of the European Union.

At the end there are two issues to return to. One is that of pragmatic responsibility. The lesson that the young David Jenkins learned when he joined the Wales TUC was that the task of trade unions is to secure for the members practical and immediate benefits rather than to prepare for the revolution. It is a philosophy wholly in line with TUC understanding of the realities of power and the need to compromise. It was George Woodcock who famously declared: 'Above all in this business we need flexibility. We need – I am not ashamed of the phrase at all – room for those shoddy, shabby, dirty compromises which are the essence of practical people trying to do a job.'[22] It is an attitude that enables the WTUC to deal willingly with governments of whatever shade – Tory, Labour or Lib–Lab – and to make progress in its aims. However, it has been a defining characteristic of the Wales TUC that it has always been able to be independent and speak as a sometimes friendly critic. It did not, in the 1970s, hesitate to criticize the governments of Wilson and Callaghan when it felt that it was necessary to do so. In these days of social partnership, when crucially important decisions can be made at a remote distance from ordinary members, it will be essential to maintain their loyalty and trust.

The other issue is the impending transformation in the governance of the United Kingdom. In the not too distant future there will be regional assemblies in parts of England. The locus and distribution of power within the British trade union movement have always responded to the changing economic and political environment. Power accrued to the TUC in the 1960s and 1970s when governments through planning bodies and incomes policies intervened in industrial and economic relationships. Power accrued at the same time to shopfloor bargainers because full employment and payment systems gave them the opportunity to raise earnings. Devolution and regionalization will soon require trade unions and the TUC to consider whether sufficient resources have been devolved to their regions to enable the unions to play a full role in regional governance. For Wales, as in Scotland, it is serious politics. The test will come when a government of a different political persuasion from that in Cardiff Bay sits in Westminster. Devolution provides the trade union movement with a challenge that is so new it is hard to grasp. The days of running to London are over. Towards the end of his life Aneurin Bevan said of the British working class, 'History gave them the chance – and they didn't take it.' It stands as a rebuke and a challenge.

Notes

1. All Change

1   Brinley Thomas (ed.), *The Welsh Economy: Studies in Expansion* (Cardiff, 1962).

2   H. A. Clegg, *The Changing System of Industrial Relations in Great Britain* (Oxford, 1979), 328–38; Richard Hyman, 'Trade unions: structure, policies, and politics' in George Sayers Bain (ed.), *Industrial Relations in Britain* (Oxford, 1983), 54–7.

3   Ross M. Martin, *TUC: The Growth of a Pressure Group 1868–1976* (Oxford, 1980), 278–9 and 291. TUC *Annual Report* (1954) contains a summary of the history and functions of the RACs, 108–11, and see also the debate, ibid., 329–31.

4   Eric Silver, *Victor Feather TUC* (London, 1973), 95–102; Richard Stevens, 'Containing radicalism: the Trades Union Congress organisation department and trades councils 1928–1953', *Labour History Review*, 62, 1 (Spring 1997).

5   Accounts of the strike and the background to it are in John Mathews, *Ford Strike: The Workers' Story* (London, 1972) and Huw Beynon, *Working for Ford* (Harmondsworth, 1973). See also *British Journal of Industrial Relations*, 9, 2 (July 1971), 260–1.

6   Clegg, *Changing System*, 51–3.

7   Moss Evans quoted in Beynon, *Working for Ford*, 308.

8   See, for example, Graham Humphrys, *Industrial Britain: South Wales* (Newton Abbot, 1972); Kenneth O. Morgan, *Rebirth of a Nation: Wales 1880–1980* (Oxford, 1981); K. D. George and Lynn Mainwaring (eds), *The Welsh Economy* (Cardiff, 1988); Gareth Rees, 'Uneven development, state intervention and the generation of inequality: the case of industrial south Wales', in Gareth Rees and Teresa Rees (eds), *Poverty and Social Inequality in Wales* (London, 1980); Victoria Winckler, 'Women and work in contemporary Wales', *Contemporary Wales*, 1 (1987).

9   G. S. Bain and Robert Price, 'Union growth: dimensions, determinants and destiny', in George Sayers Bain (ed.), *Industrial Relations in Britain* (Oxford, 1983), 27–9; William Brown, *The Changing Contours of British Industrial Relations* (Oxford, 1981), chap. 4.

10 C. McGlashan, 'A minority looking for a miracle', *Observer*, Colour Supplement (30 October 1966).

11 E. Owen Smith, *Productivity Bargaining: A Case Study in the Steel Industry* (London, 1971).

12 George and Mainwaring, *The Welsh Economy*, 162; Hywel Francis and David Smith, *The Fed* (London, 1980), 448–53.

13 K. O. Morgan, *Rebirth of a Nation*, 337; George and Mainwaring, *Welsh Economy*, 123.

14 Ithel Davies, *A Trade Union Congress for Wales* (Cardiff, n. d.); Gwyn A. Williams, *When was Wales?* (Harmondsworth, 1985), 274.

[15] NUM South Wales Area Council, *Annual Report* (1965–6); Minutes of the north and south Wales RACs, Modern Records Centre, University of Warwick. John Osmond, *Creative Conflict: The Politics of Welsh Devolution* (Llandysul, 1977), 116–19, describes some of these moves.

[16] Tom Jones, reported in *Western Mail* (6 December, 1966); NUM South Wales Area Council, *Annual Report* (1966–7).

[17] *Western Mail* (4 June 1968).

[18] TUC, *Annual Report* (1970), 557.

[19] Quoted in Osmond, *Creative Conflict*, 119. D. Ivor Davies, although small in stature was a substantial trade union figure in Wales, devoting himself to the voluntary side of the movement. A member of the Communist Party, in addition to his tireless work for trades councils he was extremely active within NUPE and became its national president. He was employed as the secretary for the Mid-Glamorgan group of hospitals.

[20] David Francis Papers, C1, Archive, Swansea University College Library; Minutes of annual meeting south Wales RAC, 26 November 1971, Modern Records Centre, Warwick University.

[21] Robert Taylor, *The TUC from the General Strike to New Unionism* (London, 2000), 202.

[22] R. Undy, 'The devolution of bargaining levels and responsibilities in the T&GWU, 1965–75', *Industrial Relations Journal*, 9, 3; R. Undy, V. Ellis, W. McCarthy and A. Halmos, *Change in Trade Unions: The Development of UK Unions since the 1960s* (London, 1981); Robert Taylor, *The TUC*, chap. 6.

[23] Interview with the author, 30 September 2002. See also Jack Jones, *Union Man: An Autobiography* (London, 1986), 200.

[24] Interview, 30 September 2002.

[25] Alan Burge, 'Miners' learning in the South Wales Coalfield 1900–1947', *Llafur*, 8 , 1 (2000), 83.

[26] On Law see Paul Smith, *Unionization and Union Leadership: The Road Haulage Industry* (London, 2001); on Wright see chap. 2.

[27] A petition with some 1,500 signatures was sent to Vic Feather as general secretary of the TUC asking him to ensure that Saunders resigned as secretary of the south Wales RAC.

[28] Interview, 30 September 2002.

[29] Tom Jones papers, Clwyd Record Office, D/JO/138.

2. *The Confrontation*

[1] Obituaries of Francis appeared on 1 April 1981 in *The Times* and the *Western Mail*. An obituary of Jones appeared in *Llafur*, 5, 4 (1991).

[2] On this dispute see Dave Lyddon, 'The car industry, 1945–79: shop stewards and workplace unionism', in Chris Wrigley (ed.), *A History of British Industrial Relations, 1939–1979* (Cheltenham, 1996); and the contribution by Dick Etheridge in R. A. Leeson, *Strike: A Live History 1887–1971* (London, 1973), 196–8.

3   On the significance of region 5 for the government of the TGWU see R. Undy et al., *Change in Trade Unions: The Development of UK Unions since the 1960s* (London, 1981), 98–100.

4   Quotations by Wright, unless otherwise noted, from interview with the author, 20 November 2002.

5   Interview with the author, 21 February 2003.

6   George Wright to J. Ellis, area secretary, north Wales NUM, 19 October 1972; Wales TUC Papers, NLW Box 1, A1.

7   Victor Feather to Tom Jones, 13 November 1972.

8   George Wright to Victor Feather, 20 November 1972.

9   Victor Feather to J. L. Jones 27 November 1972.

10 J. L. Jones to Victor Feather, 13 December 1972.

11 Tom Jones to Victor Feather, 15 December 1972.

12 TUC Circular No. 97 (1972–3), 24 January 1973.

13 TUC, *Report* (1969), 481–91.

14 TUC, *Report* (1970), 531–2.

15 TUC, *Report* (1971), 43–4.

16 TUC, *Report* (1972), 320.

17 George Wright to Victor Feather, 2 February 1973.

18 Victor Feather to George Wright, 7 February 1973.

19 John Morris, MP, to George Wright. No date but received on 12 February 1973. Morris was Parliamentary Secretary at the Ministry of Power 1964–6, Joint Parliamentary Secretary at the Ministry of Transport 1966–8 and at the Ministry of Defence (Equipment) 1968–70.

20 Tal Lloyd to George Wright, 20 March 1973, 'I am attempting to influence our Districts in pressing our Executive Council in being more definite in their support . . . up to the present, Merthyr, Swansea, and Llanelli Districts have declared themselves in support, the remainder I hope will make up their minds within the next couple of weeks.'

21 TUC Circular No. 119 (1972–3).

22 Quotations from the note of the meeting enclosed with a letter from V. Feather to the chairmen and secretaries of RACs and trades councils federations in Wales, 22 June 1973.

23 D. Ivor Davies to George Wright, 29 June 1973.

24 Wright to L. Murray, 5 July 1973; Wright to J. L. Jones and C. H. Urwin, 5 July 1973.

25 L. Murray to the chairmen and secretaries of RACs and trades council federations in Wales, 1 August 1973, with attachment.

26 Interview with the author, 24 February 2003.

27 The TUC account of proceedings is in TUC, *Report* (1973), 356–76. See also the debate, ibid., 447–54. In a note to the TUC finance and general purposes committee meeting of 23 February 1987 the then general secretary, Norman Willis, wrote: 'The formation of the WTUC led to the creation a year or so later of the English Regional Councils.'

28 The 259 delegates comprised 189 from trade unions, 56 from trades councils and 14 from the county associations of trades councils, bodies that had replaced the former trades council federations.

3. A Campaigning Organization

1   TUC, *Report* (1975), 346–64, 'The development of the social contract'.
2   TUC, *Report* (1976), 404–15, 'The social contract 1976–77'.
3   In the throes of bringing the organization into being, George Wright argued
    this point to Jack Jones: 'You will note that the Wales Trade Union Congress
    would be heavily dependant [sic] for premises and equipment upon our own
    Union, and we would therefore have control of it.' George Wright to Jack
    Jones, 31 January 1973.
4   Anthony Wedgwood Benn to George Wright, 5 August 1974, Dai Francis
    Papers, C6, South Wales Coalfield Archive, University College, Swansea. As
    chairman of the Labour Party in 1972 Benn had been largely responsible for
    the party's 1973 programme which had discussed the provision of 'money for
    unions to sponsor their own research on job problems'.
5   Agreement between the Secretary of State for Industry, the Trade Union
    Research Unit at Ruskin College, and the Wales TUC, dated 6 October 1975.
6   Denis Gregory in interview with the author, 22 November 1994.
7   Tony Benn, *Against the Tide: Diaries 1973–76* (London, 1989), 191, 211, 232, 238,
    296–7, 333.
8   Minutes of the Fourth Meeting of the General Council of the Wales TUC held
    on Wednesday 11 December 1974.
9   The TUC had reaffirmed its objection to taking public funds 'for any purpose'
    as late as 1969, see TUC, *Report* (1969), 292. John Holford, *Union Education in
    Britain* (Nottingham, 1994), 97–107, discusses the TUC's reasons for asking for
    public funds. David Lea was opposed to the TUC taking money for
    education. So was Ken Graham, head of the organization department, who
    said: 'We'll be taking money for ballots next!' TUC, *Report* (1975), 50–1, gives
    the TUC's version of events which includes providing the Wales TUC with
    permission to 'proceed with the research project as an experimental measure'.
10 Wales TUC, *Second Annual Report* (1975), 110–17.
11 For a discussion of the significance of 'authority' in relation to the TUC see
    Ross M. Martin, *TUC: The Growth of a Pressure Group 1868–1976* (Oxford,
    1980), particularly chaps 1 and 11.
12 George and Mainwaring (eds), *The Welsh Economy* (Cardiff, 1988), 207–8.
13 See the scathing critique in R. A. Bryer, T. J. Brignall, and A. R. Maunders,
    Accounting for British Steel (Aldershot, 1982); George and Mainwaring, *The
    Welsh Economy*, 221–4.
14 *Western Mail* (14 August 1975); Minutes of General Council, 10 September
    1975; *Financial Times* (27 October 1975).
15 British Steel Corporation, 'Joint Statement on Reductions in Employment
    Costs and Improvements in Labour Productivity', 23 January 1976.
16 Minutes of General Council, 10 March and 26 May 1976.
17 Wales TUC, *Third Annual Report* (1976), 67.
18 Wales TUC, *Fourth Annual Report*, (1977), 94–115.
19 Looking back at his time as Chancellor of the Exchequer, Denis Healey wrote:
    'Politically, by far the most difficult part of my ordeal was the continual

reduction of public spending; almost all of the spending cuts ran against the Labour Party's principles, and many also ran against our campaign promises.' Denis Healey, *The Time of My Life* (Harmondsworth, 1990), 401.

20 His strategic document was widely leaked and published as 'Appomattox or Civil War?', *The Economist* (27 May 1978).

21 NLW, Wales TUC Archive, Box 63, G2/11/2/1.

22 *Financial Times* (12, 13, 15, 18, 19 December 1979); WTUC General Council Minutes, 19 December 1979.

23 TUC, *Report* (1980), 273; Lionel Murray to George Wright, 24 January 1980.

24 *Financial Times* (18 January 1980); *The Times* (30 January 1980); *Guardian* (16 February 1980).

25 House of Commons, Committee on Welsh Affairs, *The Role of the Welsh Office and Associated Bodies in Developing Employment Opportunities in Wales*, vol. 2 (London, 1980), 573; *Western Mail* (9 July 1980).

26 House of Commons, Committee on Welsh Affairs, *The Role of the Welsh Office and Associated Bodies in Developing Employment Opportunities in Wales*, vol. 1 (London, 1980).

27 Bill Sirs, *Hard Labour* (London, 1984), 98. In this volume Sirs gives an account of the steel strike from an ISTC perspective.

28 See TUC, *Report* (1980), 273–5.

29 Wales TUC, Report of Special General Council Meeting, 6 February 1980.

30 *Guardian* (16 February 1980); *Financial Times* (16 and 20 February 1980).

31 Wales TUC, *Seventh Annual Report* (1980), 204–10.

32 Wales TUC, Minutes of General Council Meeting, 15 October 1980.

33 TUC, *Report* (1981), 296–7.

34 Sirs, *Hard Labour*, 69.

35 M. Upham, 'British Steel: retrospect and prospect', *Industrial Relations Journal* (July/August 1980); Sirs, 'Redundancy payments in the BSC – a lesson for the rail industry?', *Locomotive Journal* (August 1981).

36 Wales TUC Research Unit Papers: *The Social Consequences of Steel Closures in Wales* (1974); *Social and Economic Aspects of the Planned Closure at Ebbw Vale Steelworks* (April 1976); *The Deeside Economy: Results and Prospects* (July 1976).

37 Sirs, *Hard Labour*, 85; and letter in *Rebecca* (June 1982).

38 P. Cosgrave, *Thatcher: The First Term* (London, 1985), 226; Hugo Young, *One of us* (London, 1990), 225–6.

39 Young, *One of us*, 198–204; Jim Prior, *A Balance of Power* (London, 1986), 118–26.

40 Bryer et al., *Accounting*, section 5.

41 In July 1980 the ISTC acting alone published an 'alternative strategy', *New Deal for Steel*. It was, however, too little too late.

4.   *The Enemy Within?*

1 Quoted in John McIlroy, 'Ten years for the locust: the TUC in the 1980s', in D. Cox (ed.), *Facing the Future* (Nottingham, 1992).

[2] Wales TUC, *Ninth Annual Report* (1982), 103–58.

[3] Mrs Thatcher, 20 July 1984. Quoted in Andrew J. Richards, *Miners on Strike: Class Solidarity and Division in Britain* (Oxford, 1996), 117.

[4] P. Davies and M. Freedland, *Labour Legislation and Public Policy* (Oxford, 1993).

[5] Sir K. Joseph, *Conditions for Fuller Employment* (London, 1979), 2.

[6] W. Brown, S. Deakin, D. Nash and S. Oxenbridge, 'The employment contract: from collective procedures to individual rights', *British Journal of Industrial Relations*, 38, (2000).

[7] Jim Prior, *A Balance of Power* (London, 1986), 126.

[8] Colin Crouch, 'Review essay', *Historical Studies in Industrial Relations*, 2 (September 1996), 120.

[9] For south Wales see Hywel Francis and Gareth Rees, ' "No surrender in the Valleys": the 1984–5 miners' strike in south Wales', *Llafur*, 5, 2 (1989); for south Wales and Yorkshire see Andrew J. Richards, *Miners on Strike: Class Solidarity and Division in Britain* (Oxford, 1996); more generally, see Hywel Francis, 'NUM united: a team in disarray', *Marxism Today*, 29, 4 (April 1985); Martin Adeney and John Lloyd, *The Miners' Strike 1984–5: Loss without Limit* (London, 1986).

[10] *Sunday Times* (28 October 1984), quoted in Michael Crick, *Scargill and the Miners* (Harmondsworth, 1985), 140.

[11] Richards, *Miners on Strike*, 138–9.

[12] Kim Howells, 'Stopping out: the birth of a new kind of politics', in Huw Beynon (ed.), *Digging Deeper: Issues in the Miners' Strike* (London, 1985), 144.

[13] Francis and Rees, 'No surrender', 66.

[14] Quoted by Hywel Francis in 'NUM united'.

[15] Wales TUC, *Seventh Annual Report* (1980), 205.

[16] General secretary's report to the general council, 20 June 1979.

[17] WTUC Archive, NLW. Box E/72; interview with the author, 17 January 1985.

[18] TUC, *Annual Report* (1963).

[19] Hugo Young, *One of us* (London, 1990), 369.

[20] Denis Gregory, *The Welsh Economy in the Post-War Period: A Programme for Economic Reconstruction* (Cardiff, 1993).

[21] George Wright, interview 18 July 2003.

[22] See the contemporary publications of the Institute for Workers' Control; Michael Poole, *Workers' Participation in Industry* (London, 1975 and 1978); *The Report of the Committee of Inquiry on Industrial Democracy* (Cmnd. 6706, London, 1977); and Robert Oakeshott, *The Case for Workers' Co-ops* (London, 1978).

[23] Wales TUC, *Wales at the* Abyss, appendix B; Wales TUC, *Seventh Annual Report* (1980), 46.

[24] H. Thomas and C. Logan, *Mondragon: An Economic Analysis* (London, 1980).

[25] Chris Logan and Denis Gregory, *Co-operation and Job Creation in Wales: A Feasibility Study* (Cardiff, 1981).

[26] Wales TUC, *Tenth Annual Report* (1983), 49; *Eleventh Annual Report* (1984), 47.

[27] Wales TUC, *Twelfth Annual Report* (1985), 130–3.

28   Wales Co-operative Centre, *Annual Reports* (1985–6 and 1987).

29   Interview with author, 29 August 2003.

30   Wales TUC Archive, NLW, 18 D3/1.

31   Wales TUC Archive, NLW, G1/10/1, letter 31 October 1978.

32   This paragraph based upon the memorandum submitted by the Development Corporation for Wales to the Committee for Welsh Affairs, First Report, *The Role of the Welsh Office and Associated Bodies in Developing Employment Opportunities in Wales*, vol. 2 (London, 1980).

33   'The Employment Policies of Overseas Inward Investors in Wales', *Industrial Relations Review and Report* (22 February 1991).

34   David Jenkins in interview with the author, 16 February 1995.

35   *South Wales Echo* (5 June 1980); Wales TUC, General Council Minutes, 18 June 1980; Wales TUC, *Seventh Annual Report*, 69–70.

36   Wales TUC Archive, NLW, G1/10/1.

37   There were limits to such collaboration. In the summer of 1981 a meeting with Edwards seemed to indicate 'for the first time a clear desire . . . to involve the Wales TUC in tackling the economic and social problems within the Principality'. Edwards specifically invited the Wales TUC to itemize and prioritize those items of capital expenditure that the government might introduce or bring forward. Fearful of the internal disagreements that might follow such a response the general council advised the Secretary of State to bring forward *all* his capital programmes (Wales TUC, General Council Minutes, 19 August 1981).

38   See Minutes of Economic and Industrial Committee, 25 July 1977.

39   Information from George Wright; also Wales TUC, 'Wales TUC and inward investment', paper prepared for March 1987 general council; see also David Jenkins, 'What about the Workers!', a statement to potential inward investors; and ACAS, *Successful Industrial Relations: The Experience of Overseas Companies in Wales* (ACAS, Cardiff, 1986), appendix 2.

40   William Brown (ed.), *The Changing Contours of British Industrial Relations* (Oxford, 1981), 59.

41   Wales TUC Archive, NLW, G1/10/1, letter from Harry Harris to George Wright, 4 March 1981. See also Wright's response dated 10 March: 'The points set out clearly confirm completely the attitude I would have adopted and the general approach from the Wales TUC.'

42   Kevin Morgan, *The Fallible Servant* (Cardiff, 1994), 18–19.

43   David Jenkins in interview with author, 16 February 1995.

44   George Wright, interview 18 July 2003. The ACAS report, *Successful Industrial Relations*, noted: 'In the main, however, full recognition of a trade union had become the norm in our sample, with incoming companies accepting, in a pragmatic and proactive way, the positive role that trade unions have played in Wales.'

45   K. Morgan and A. Sayer, 'The international electronics industry and regional development in Britain', in Wales TUC, *Tenth Annual Report* (1983), 110–19; Jonathan Morris, Barry Wilkinson and Max Munday, 'Towards a new unionism? The deal, the company, the union and the member', conference paper 1993.

46   *Financial Times* (18 January 1988); and John Allen and Doreen Massey (eds), *The Economy in Question* (London, 1988), 179–81.

[47]   Useful discussions of the influx of Japanese firms into Wales are in Kevin
       Morgan and Andrew Sayer, 'A modern industry in a mature region', *International Journal of Urban and Regional Research*, 9, 3 (September 1985);
       M. Munday, *Japanese Manufacturing Investment in Wales* (Cardiff, 1990); Barry
       Wilkinson, Jonathan Morris and Max Munday, 'Japan in Wales: a new IR',
       Industrial Relations Journal, 24, 4 (December 1993).
[48]   William Brown, 'The changing role of trade unions in the management of
       labour', *British Journal of Industrial Relations*, 24, 2 (July 1986).

5. New Directions

[1]   Interviews with author, 18 January 1995, 16 February 1995, 8 October 2003.
[2]   John Osmond, *The Democratic Challenge* (Llandysul, 1992); Kevin Morgan and
      Ellis Roberts, *The Democratic Deficit: A Guide to Quangoland* (Cardiff, 1993).
[3]   Reviews of the Welsh economy and relevant statistics are in successive issues
      of *Contemporary Wales* (University of Wales Press, Cardiff, 1987–).
[4]   Graham Humphrys, *Industrial Britain: South Wales* (Newton Abbot, 1972);
      George and Mainwaring (eds), *The Welsh Economy* (Cardiff, 1988).
[5]   David Brooksbank and Stephen Drinkwater, 'The Welsh economy: a statistical profile', *Contemporary Wales*, 11 (1998), 223–4; David Brooksbank, 'The
      Welsh economy: a statistical profile', *Contemporary Wales*, 14 (2001), 173–4.
[6]   David Blackaby, Philip Murphy, Nigel O'Leary and Eirian Thomas, 'Wales: an
      economic survey', *Contemporary Wales*, 8 (1995), 270–1.
[7]   Victoria Winckler, 'Women and work in contemporary Wales', *Contemporary
      Wales*, 1 (1987).
[8]   P. Bassett and A. Cave, *All for One: The Future of the Unions* (London, 1993).
[9]   Jeremy Waddington and Colin Whitston, 'Trade unions: growth, structure
      and policy', in Paul Edwards (ed.), *Industrial Relations: Theory and Practice in
      Britain* (Oxford, 1995).
[10] Philip Bassett, *Strike Free: New Industrial Relations in Britain* (London, 1987).
[11] TUC, *Report* (1985), 6–8.
[12] TUC, *The EETPU Suspension: A TUC Information Note* (1988); TUC, *Annual
      Report* (1988), 22–7, 338–92, 404–11.
[13] Barry Wilkinson, Jonathan Morris and Max Munday, 'Japan in Wales: a new
      IR' *Industrial Relations Journal*, 24, 4 (December 1993).
[14] *South Wales Echo* (1 May 1987).
[15] D. H. Simpson, *Manufacturing Industry in Wales: Prospects for Employment
      Growth* (Cardiff, 1987).
[16] TUC, *Report* (1988), 568–70.
[17] Edmund Heery, 'The relaunch of the Trades Union Congress', *British Journal
      of Industrial Relations*, 36, 3 (September 1998).
[18] Wales TUC, *The Economy of Wales: Our Present and Future Needs* (Submission
      to the Government on Friday, 10 October 1975).
[19] David Jenkins, 'Towards full employment in Wales', *Welsh Agenda*, 1, 2 (April 1995).

20 Eileen Smith, 'Political Annie's off again', *Moving Left in Wales* (Summer 1983).

21 I. Boraston, H. Clegg and M. Rimmer, *Workplace and Union* (London, 1975), 63–4.

22 This innovation was the result of a report commissioned by the union's national executive. See Bob Fryer, Andy Fairclough and Tom Manson, *Organisation and Change in the National Union of Public Employees* (Warwick, 1974).

23 Wales TUC, *Thirteenth Annual Report* (1986), 18–20.

24 Issues pertaining to race in Wales are discussed in Charlotte Williams, Neil Evans and Paul O'Leary (eds), *A Tolerant Nation? Exploring Ethnic Diversity in Wales* (Cardiff, 2003).

25 Wales TUC, *Seventh Annual Report* (1980), 157–67.

26 A detailed account of the negotiations is contained in Wales TUC, *General Council Report of Discussions with the TUC on TUC/Wales TUC Relationships* (n.d.).

27 Interview with the author, 21 October 2003.

28 TUC, *Congress Report* (1996), chap. 16.

6. *Devolution and After*

1 John Osmond, *Creative Conflict: The Politics of Devolution* (Llandysul and London, 1977), 121.

2 Quoted ibid., 121.

3 Wales TUC, *Recommendations on Devolution* (Cardiff, n.d.).

4 For accounts of the progress towards devolution see Leighton Andrews, *Wales Says Yes* (Bridgend, 1999); J. Barry Jones and Dennis Balsom (eds), *The Road to the National Assembly for Wales* (Cardiff, 2000); and Kevin Morgan and Geoff Mungham, *Redesigning Democracy: The Making of the Welsh Assembly* (Bridgend, 2000).

5 Wales TUC, *Briefing Paper: Resources and functioning of the Wales TUC in Light of the Decision to Establish a National Assembly for Wales* (1998).

6 Wales TUC, *Economic Development and Regeneration* (2003).

7 Interview, 24 November 2003.

8 Speech by Bill Speirs, general secretary of the Scottish TUC to a Unions 21 seminar. Reported in Unions 21, *Devolution, Scotland and the Unions* (London, n.d.).

9 TUC press release, 'TUC and partners launch Regional Governance course', 5 November 2003. For discussion of these issues see TUC northern region, *Trade Unions and Regional Government* (Newcastle-upon-Tyne, 2001) and Peter O'Brien, *Devolution and the Trade Union Movement: The Key Issues* (Newcastle, 2003).

10 P. K. Edwards, *Conflict at Work* (Oxford, 1986).

11 *The Miners' Next Step* (Tonypandy, 1912).

12 Keith Gildart, *North Wales Miners: A Fragile Unity, 1945–1996* (Cardiff, 2001).

13 Office of National Statistics, *Labour Market Trends* (July 2002).

14 John Williams, *Digest of Welsh Historical Statistics*, vol. 2 (Cardiff, 1985), 97, 163.

15 E. Heery, 'The Relaunch of the Trades Union Congress', *British Journal of Industrial Relations*, 36, 3. See also Peter Fairbrother and Paul Stewart, 'The

dilemmas of social partnership and union organization: questions for British trade unions', in Peter Fairbrother and Charlotte A. B. Yates (eds), *Trade Unions in Renewal: A Comparative Study* (London, 2003); Richard Hyman, *Understanding European Trade Unionism: Between Market, Class and Society* (London, 2001).

[16] Howard Gospel and Stephen Wood (eds), *Representing Workers: Union Recognition and Membership in Britain* (London, 2003), 13.

[17] See the publications of the ESRC's Future of Work Programme, particularly those by Robert Taylor available at *www.leeds.ac.uk/esrcfutureofwork*.

[18] Interview with author, 5 November 2003.

[19] Alan Flanders, 'Trade unions in the sixties', *Socialist Commentary* (August 1961); reprinted in Alan Flanders, *Management and Unions: The Theory and Reform of Industrial Relations* (London, 1970).

[20] Victoria Winckler, *Ambitions for the Future* (Tredegar, 2003); Welsh Assembly Government, *People, Places, Futures: the Wales Spatial Plan* (Cardiff, 2003); Wales TUC, *Annual Report 1992–3*.

[21] Interview with author, 15 December 2003.

[22] Sarah Oxenbridge and William Brown, 'The two faces of partnership? An assessment of partnership and co-operative employer/trade union relationships', *Employee Relations* (2002).

[23] Trades Union Congress, *Report 1967*, 539–40.

Appendix 1

Papers Produced by the Wales TUC Research Unit, March 1975–December 1977

Transport in Wales	March 1975
Removal of the Lump	March 1975
Housing in Wales	March 1975
Unemployment in Wales: Problems and Prospects	June 1975
Local Authority Expenditure Cuts	September 1975
The Economy of Wales: Our Present and Future Needs	October 1975
Encouraging Regional Investment	November 1975
Women at Work in Wales	January 1976
A Note on the Shortage of Training Opportunities for Young Persons in Wales	January 1976
Powys: The Economic Outlook	February 1976
Social and Economic Aspects of the Planned Closure At Ebbw Vale Steelworks	April 1976
Young Persons' Unemployment in Wales	May 1976
Industrial Accidents and Ill-health in Wales	May 1976
Notes on the Future of the Coal Industry in Wales	May 1976
Wentloog Development and the Economy of South Glam.	June 1976
The Deeside Economy: Results and Prospects	July 1976
Recent Developments in Unemployment in Wales	August 1976
'Into Work': A Proposal for a Linked Employment and Training Programme for Young Persons	August 1976
Health and Safety at Work in Wales	October 1976
Critical Aspects of Economic Development in Wales	October 1976
Financial Implication of the Strategy for the Regeneration of the Valleys	November 1976
Wales TUC Economic Review	April 1977
Unemployment: The Way Out, A Ten-Year Strategy	December 1977

Index

AB Electronics 88
Abbey steelworks 8
Aberdare 7
Abergavenny 9
Aberystwyth 31, 32, 33, 34, 35
Advisory, Conciliation and Arbitration
    Services (ACAS) 37
Aiwa 88
Allen, Alf 32
Amalgamated Engineering and
    Electrical Union (AEEU) 86, 89
Amalgamated Engineering Union
    (AEU) 20, 28, 39, 87
Amalgamated Union of Engineering
    Workers (AUEW) 71, 75, 86, 88, 94
AMICUS 86
Association of Professional, Executive,
    Clerical and Computer Staff
    (APEX) 88
Association of Scientific, Technical and
    Managerial Staff (ASTMS) 28, 39,
    86, 88
Atkinson, John 40, 68, 81
Austin–Crompton Parkinson 7

Barber, Brendan 101, 102
Beeching Report (1963) 9
Benn, Tony 39, 40, 46
Beswick, Lord 39, 43
Bevan, Aneurin 51, 120
Bevan Foundation 117
Bevan, Wyn 89
Bevin, Ernest 13, 27
Biffen, John 57
Blackwood 7
Borg–Warner 7

Bridgend 6
British Airways 60
British Leyland 60
British Steel Corporation (BSC) 43, 44,
    46, 47, 48, 50, 53–6, 57
Britton, Edward 32
Brooks, Jack 28
Brynmawr 6

Caernarfon 7, 28
Callaghan, James 38, 45, 81
Cardiff 7, 32, 33, 38, 45, 49, 54, 62, 80,
    99, 105
car workers 4–5, 18, 102
Christian Salvesen 89
Clerical and Administrative Workers'
    Union (CAWU) 11, 15
Clwyd, Anne 50
coal industry 6, 7, 9–10, 14, 42, 85, 90
Communication Workers' Union
    (CWU) 86
Communist Party 4, 10, 17,
Confederation of British Industry
    (CBI) Wales 72, 73, 92, 98, 105, 108
Conservative Party 1
    Heath government 4, 14, 15, 35, 43
    Macmillan government 7
    Thatcher government 38, 46, 58–61,
        90–1, 112
Courtaulds 45
Cousins, Frank 13, 27
Cwmbran 7

Daly, Lawrence 22, 26, 49
Davies, D. Ivor 11, 12, 33, 34
Davies, D. J. 28

Davies, Ron 64
Deakin, Arthur 17, 27
Delors, Jacques 90
Development Board for Rural Wales
  (DBRW) 1, 69
devolution 1, 2, 35, 38, 39, 41, 64,
  102–8, 110–11, 118, 120
Distribution of Industry Act (1945) 6
Dunlop 6, 8

Ebbw Vale 8, 45, 88, 95
Edwards, Nicholas 51, 65–6, 72
Electrical, Electronic,
  Telecommunications and Plumbing
  Union (EETPU) 77, 78, 86, 87–9
Employment Acts (1980, 1982, 1988,
  1989 and 1990) 59, 87
Employment Protection Act (1975) 37
Employment Relations Act (1999) 91
Enfield Clocks 6
Equal Opportunities Commission
  (EOC) 94, 96, 109
Equal Pay Act (1970) 95
European Economic Community
  (EEC) 41, 42, 43, 50, 99, 100
European Parliament 67, 99
European Social Fund 69
European Union (EU) 117, 119
Evans, Moss 4, 15, 18, 80

Feather, Victor 2, 33
  negotiations for a Wales TUC 21–32
Ferodo 7
Fforestfach 6
Fisher and Ludlow 7
Flint 45
Foot, Michael 45, 49
Ford Motor Company 4, 5, 7, 8, 38
Francis, Dai 12, 15, 16, 17, 18, 20–1, 35,
  39, 58

GEC 88
General, Municipal and Boilermakers'
  Union (GMB) 86, 87, 88
General and Municipal Workers'
  Union (GMWU) 28, 85–6
George, Ken 39
Government of Wales Act (1998) 104
GPMU 86

Graham, Ken 32
Greene, Sid 30
Gregory, Denis 40, 58, 68, 81
Griffiths, John 72
Guinness, Sir Alec 64

Hague, William 66
Hammond, Eric 88
Health and Safety at Work Act (1974)
  37
Heathfield, Peter 61
Heseltine, Michael 90
Hirwaun 6, 9, 41
Hitachi 88
Hoover 6, 8, 94
Hotpoint 7
Howe, Sir Geoffrey 49
Howell, Fred 32
Howells, Kim 62
Hughes, Cledwyn 31
Hunt, Lord Crowther 39
Hunt, David 66

ICI Nylon Spinners 6, 8
Industrial Relations Act (1971) 3, 14,
  37
Inland Revenue Staff Association
  (IRSF) 12, 20
Inmos 88
inward investment 70–3, 76–8, 83, 87,
  89, 93, 112, 115
Iron and Steel Trades Confederation
  (ISTC) 47, 48, 49, 56, 62, 86, 87

Jackson, Tom 25
Japanese companies 71, 74, 77, 78, 87–9
Jenkins, Clare 116
Jenkins, David 65, 69, 73, 80–2, 85, 90,
  93, 97, 105, 110, 118, 119
Jones, J. Emrys 28
Jones, Jack 5, 13, 14, 15, 16, 22, 25, 26,
  27, 29, 30, 34, 35
Jones, John 20, 23, 32
Jones, Keith 28, 38, 40
Jones, Peter 20, 21, 23
Jones, Sylvia 64
Jones, Tom 11, 12, 13, 15, 16, 17, 21,
  22–3, 29, 34
Joseph, Sir Keith 46, 49, 50, 51, 60, 65

labourism 77, 112
Labour Party 1, 2, 14, 15, 16, 17, 22, 23,
    31, 58, 65, 80, 98, 103, 110
    Attlee government 6, 117
    Blair government 91, 94, 112
    Callaghan government 38, 44, 67, 119
    Wilson government 7, 35, 37, 44, 70,
        92, 119
Land Authority for Wales 1
Law, Alan 14
Lea, David 41
Liverpool University 80
Llandrindod Wells 12, 21, 24, 27, 28,
    29, 32, 33, 34, 67
Llandudno 7, 52
Llanelli 7
Lloyd, Tal 20, 28, 39

MacGregor, Ian 53
Maesteg 7
Major, John 60, 77, 90
Manpower Services Commission
    (MSC) 60, 92
manufacturing 7, 83, 109
Manufacturing, Science, Finance
    (MSF) 86, 87
Mathias, Ron 12
Merthyr Tydfil 6, 20, 67, 94
Metal Box 8
Mondragon 68
Monks, John 91, 100, 101
Morgan, Hubert 99
Morris, John 28, 31, 41, 65, 102
Morris Motors 7
Murdoch, Rupert 61, 89
Murray, Lionel (Len) 30, 31, 32, 33,
    35, 40–1, 45, 46, 51–2, 53, 58, 61, 63,
    69, 118

National Association of Schoolmasters/
    Union of Women Teachers
    (NASUWT) 86
National Association of Teachers in
    Further and Higher Education
    (NATFHE) 81
National Coal Board (NCB) 50, 51, 57
National Economic Development
    Council (NEDC) 3, 60
National Enterprise Board (NEB) 3, 60

National and Local Government
    Officers' Association (NALGO) 3,
    20, 31, 32, 86
National Union of Blastfurnacemen
    47
National Union of Mineworkers
    (NUM) 14, 16, 17, 22, 28, 34, 39, 49,
    56, 62, 63, 64, 87
    south Wales area 10, 11, 12, 14, 21,
        24, 34, 47, 52, 56, 58, 62, 63, 82, 86
National Union of Public Service
    Employees (NUPE) 58, 63, 86, 96
National Union of Railwaymen (NUR)
    30, 63
National Union of Teachers (NUT) 3,
    28, 32, 86
Newcastle University 112
nuclear power stations 8

oil refineries 8
Orion Electric 88

partnership 76–7, 91, 92, 108, 112–19
Paul, Les 12, 20, 23, 69, 99
Pembrey 6
Phillips, Glyn 20
Plaid Cymru 1, 10, 31
Plant, Cyril 32
Pontypool 6
Port Talbot 8, 9, 62, 63, 88
Prior, Jim 57
Prime, Audrey 32
privatization 60
Public and Commercial Services Union
    (PCS) 86

Race Discrimination Act (1976) 37
Race Relations Acts (1968 and 1976)
    95
racial equality 96–7
Read Transport 63
Redwood, John 66
Rees, George 23, 50, 64
Revlon 7
Rhoose airport 41, 42
Richard, Ivor 69
Ridley, Sir Nicholas 46
RMT 86
Robeson, Paul Jnr 97

Saltley Marsh Coal Depot 14, 15
Saunders, Graham 11, 15, 30
Scargill, Arthur 61, 63
service sector 83, 93, 116, 119
Severn Bridge 9, 54
Sex Discrimination Act (1975) 37, 95
  (1986) 59
Shaw, Eleri 38
shop stewards 4, 5, 7, 8, 18, 28, 78, 95, 96
Simpson, David 89
single-union agreements 73–8, 87–9
Sirs, Bill 49, 55, 56
Social Charter 90
Social Contract 37, 112
Social Security Pensions Act (1975) 37
South Wales Miners' Federation 6, 10,
  14, 113
Sports Council for Wales 1
steel and tinplate industries 6, 7, 8, 9,
  36, 42–57, 85, 114
  Briton Ferry 42, 45
  Brymbo 42
  East Moors 8, 9, 42, 43, 45, 67, 68
  Ebbw Vale 8, 9, 42, 43, 68
  Gowerton 42
  Llanelli 42, 55
  Llanwern 8, 42, 43, 46, 47, 53, 62,
  63
  Margam, Port Talbot 9, 42, 43, 45,
  46, 53, 56, 63
  see also Abbey steelworks
  Shotton 8, 9, 42, 43, 45, 46, 56, 64,
  67, 68
  Trostre 8, 46
  Velindre 8, 46
strikes 4, 5, 14, 35, 38, 47–8, 49, 56–7,
  95, 113
  coal (1984–85) 61–4, 75
  steel (1980) 47–53, 56
Swansea 4, 5, 7,

Technical, Administrative and
  Supervisory Staffs (TASS) 86, 88
Thatcher, Margaret 46, 57, 61, 64, 65,
  76, 77, 78, 90, 110
Thomas, Brinley 1
Thomas, Dafydd Elis 46
Todd, Ron 80
Tower Colliery 70

Trade Union Act (1984) 59
Trade Union and Labour Relations
  (Consolidation) Act (1992) 59, 87
Trade Union and Labour Relations
  Acts (1974 and 1976) 37
trade union membership 82–7, 114–15
Trade Union Reform and Employment
  Rights Act (1993) 59
Trade Union Research Unit (TURU) 40
trades councils 3, 4, 8, 10, 11, 12, 17, 23,
  28, 30, 32, 33–4, 118
Trades Union Congress (TUC) 2, 3, 4,
  12, 17, 22, 24–6, 29–33, 35, 38, 40–1,
  47, 50–3, 55–6, 57, 60–1, 63, 69, 70,
  81, 82, 88, 90–1, 112, 120
  General Council 3, 10, 17, 24–6, 27,
  32, 34, 48, 49, 91, 100
  Regional Advisory Council (RAC)
  3, 4, 8, 11, 12, 15, 21, 22, 23, 24–5,
  27, 28, 30, 31, 39
training 92–4
Training Commission 92–3
Training and Enterprise Council (TEC) 93
Transport and General Workers' Union
  (TGWU) 4, 5, 8, 13, 14, 16, 17, 18–19,
  23–4, 28, 32, 34, 38, 39, 47, 49, 62, 80,
  82, 85, 86, 87, 95, 97, 99
Tredegar 7
Treforest 6

Union of Construction, Allied Trades
  and Technicians (UCATT) 88
unemployment 6, 7, 9, 10, 42, 44,
  59–60, 66, 72, 82, 92, 115
union mergers 85–6
Union of Shop Distributive and Allied
  Workers (USDAW) 20, 28, 32, 86
Unison 86, 103
Urwin, Harry 18, 19, 24, 32, 34

Velindre 8

Wages Act (1986) 59
Wales Co-operative Centre 67–70, 91
Wales plc 77
Wales Tourist Board 1
Wales TUC 1, 9, 13, 17, 30, 31, 32, 33, 34,
  38, 41, 43, 45, 49–52, 53–4, 55–7, 67,
  70–1, 86–7, 91, 107, 116, 117, 118, 119

conference 44, 52, 58, 68–9, 89, 96, 97
General Council 34, 39, 41, 47, 50, 54,
  58, 62, 72, 89, 95, 96, 97, 100, 101
Learning Services Unit 94, 107,
  108, 116
relations with TUC 42, 52–3,
  97–101, 106–7
relations with Welsh Office 41,
  64–7, 71–3, 76, 87, 89, 112
Research Unit 40, 43, 44, 45, 48, 55–6
single-union agreements 73–5, 77–9
Women's Advisory Committee 95
Wales Union Learning Fund (WULF)
  94, 108
Walker, Peter 65–6, 117
Weekes, Phillip 46, 51
Welsh Arts Council 1
Welsh Assembly Government (WAG)
  94, 102, 104, 105, 109, 112
Welsh Development Agency (WDA) 1,
  67, 69, 70, 73

Welsh Language Act (1967) 1
Welsh Office 1, 9, 10, 22, 29, 40, 41, 68,
  69, 72–3, 75, 87, 98, 104
Western Mail 11, 13, 16
white-collar jobs 8–9
Williams, Alan 71
Williams, Emlyn 23, 48, 50, 63, 82
Williams, Glyn 31
Williams, John 23
Willis, Norman 63–4, 89, 91, 100
Winter of Discontent 37, 112, 118
women 76, 85, 92, 94–6, 116
Woodcock, George 2, 11, 65, 119
Workers' Educational Association 108
Wright, George 15, 16, 18–19, 35, 40,
  41, 45, 46, 48, 49, 52, 53–4, 58, 64, 69,
  70, 80, 81, 89, 98, 99, 103
  negotiations for a Wales TUC
  19–35

Yuasa Batteries 88